Yearbook 2010

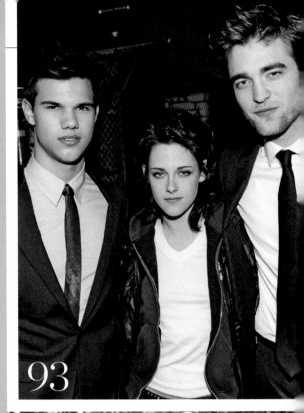

93

4

72

10

130

116

96

First Steps

A glorious Inauguration, a splendid first dance, and then: health care, tea parties, Iraq, Glenn Beck. Welcome to the Presidency

PRESIDENT
BARACK OBAMA *and*
FIRST LADY
MICHELLE OBAMA
✴
January 20, 2009

Obama Makes History

Sworn in before millions, tested by crises, President Obama has a tumultuous first year in office—and still finds time for date night

He arrived to great fanfare, quickly charmed the press but soon got booted out of the White House bedroom. First Pet Bo, a 6-month-old Portuguese water dog, was a campaign promise kept by Barack Obama, 48, who told daughters Malia and Sasha they could have a pup if he won the West Wing. Win it he did, drawing a record 1.5 million people to the Capitol for his historic Jan. 20 Inauguration (zillions more watched on TV). "First African-American President," Malia warned him before his big address. "Better be good."

How's he doing? Depends on who you ask. Obama's first year in office was a wild dash through woolly times, requiring plenty of fancy footwork—starting with 10 consecutive Inaugural balls ("How good-looking is my wife?" the new Prez said at one shindig, before slow-dancing with Michelle to "At Last"). But that was about it for the honeymoon—the worst recession in decades forced him to spend trillions bailing out banks, big insurers and automakers before he even figured out how to use the Oval Office intercom. Then Obama launched a contentious bid for health care reform, raising the Beltway's collective blood pressure (Death panels!

✳ HAIL TO THE CHIEF At Obama's Jan. 20 Inauguration (above), Michelle held the same Bible Abraham Lincoln used in 1861 (during the proceedings Sasha, far right, shot her dad a few thumbs-ups). That night, the Obamas attended 10 Inaugural Balls (left). In September, Obama turned up on *Late Night with David Letterman* (below). His daughters Malia and Sasha "basically just goofed off all summer," he told Dave, "which I couldn't do."

HOOPSTER IN CHIEF Obama (shooting around with White House staffers on Martha's Vineyard on Aug. 26) tries to work out six times a week.

Tea-baggers! Socialized medicine!). Right-wing critics complained when he vowed to close Guantanamo Bay and accused him of moving too fast in Iraq and not fast enough in Afghanistan. Along the way he mixed it up with conservative talk show hosts ("All of you voted for me," he joked at the White House correspondents' dinner. "Apologies to the Fox table."), got caught in another meaningless media kerfuffle when he bowed to the Japanese emperor, and—after rapper Kanye West interrupted Taylor Swift's speech at September's MTV Video Music Awards—was overheard on a live microphone calling Kanye a "jackass" (one statement on which an oft-divided nation could probably find common ground).

Not that Obama ever seemed to lose his cool. "I see him thriving in this," Michelle told PEOPLE. "I don't see the weight." He kept up his semiregular date nights with the wife (they took in a Broadway show in May), occasional pick-up basketball games with buddies and frequent sit-down meals with his kids. "We have dinner as a family together every night," said Michelle. "And Barack, when he's not travelling, tucks the girls in." There were victories, to be sure: He gave the Supreme Court its first Hispanic judge, Sonia Sotomayor, and in October he won a surprise Nobel Peace Prize for his efforts to "strengthen international diplomacy and cooperation between peoples"—though many called it embarrassingly premature (Obama said he was "humbled").

How, then, to sum up the start of the Obama era? Check back next year. "We have chosen hope over fear," he told a sea of citizens at his rousing Inauguration, "and unity of policy over conflict and discord." Yet about the only Obama decision that didn't get heckled was his choice of shaggy, sweet-natured Bo. "He's got star quality," said Obama of the new First Pooch. So, we were assured during his tricky first year, does the President—and he's going to need it.

✸ A FAMILY AFFAIR The Obamas want to keep their daughters "out of the [public] conversation," says Michelle, who tries to give them as normal a life as possible—and that includes having a dog, Bo (left, missing a tackle). Above, Malia and Sasha went sledding on the White House grounds March 2. At left, the First Family took in the Grand Canyon during an Aug. 16 trip. And, below, the Obamas brought their daughters with them to meet Russian President Dmitry Medvedev on July 6. "Our girls are just complete comic relief," Michelle told PEOPLE. "They're pretty funny in their observations and sort of lack of being impressed with any of this."

Farewell to the King

*The world mourns the sudden death of
pop's biggest—and most enigmatic—star*

Sequined gloves, plastic surgery, Neverland, scandal,
marriage (to Elvis's daughter, no less), kids, veils
and Bubbles the Chimp. In the longest run, none of
that may matter. "There will be a lot written about what
came next in Michael's life, but to me all of that is just
noise," said Michael Jackson's friend and collaborator,
Thriller producer Quincy Jones, shortly after the singer's
death on June 25. "I promise you, in 50, 75, 100 years,
what will be remembered is the music. It's no accident that
almost three decades later, no matter where I go in the
world, in every club and karaoke bar, like clockwork, you
hear 'Billie Jean,' 'Beat It,' "Wanna Be Startin' Something,'
'Rock with You' and 'Thriller.'"

The world agreed: Jackson's sudden death, at 50,
caused millions to mourn his loss and to celebrate—often
spontaneously, in public gatherings from Paris to Shanghai

and Buenos Aires—the gifts that had made him music's most global phenomenon. Radio stations played his greatest hits nonstop for days, fans staged mass Moonwalks, and celebrities strained to pay tribute to a man-boy who redefined the meaning of superstar. "It goes without saying, the world has lost a true musical icon," said Usher, "a man who set the bar for artists to focus on a cause bigger than themselves. I'll miss the magic that is Michael." Said Celine Dion: "It feels like when Kennedy died, when Elvis died. It's an amazing loss."

Still, despite a tsunami of love and a tele-vised memorial service broadcast worldwide and online, Jackson was at the center of another scandal. An autopsy revealed that his body contained a pharmacy of powerful drugs, including the anesthetic Propofol

and a cocktail of three powerful sedatives. The L.A. coroner ruled the death a homicide, and authorities began investigating how Jackson obtained so many drugs and who administered them to him. Investigators seized evidence from the singer's personal physician, Dr. Conrad Murray, and Jackson's dermatologist, Dr. Arnold Klein.

Jackson being Jackson, he was laid to rest as befitted the King of Pop, and as he probably would have wanted. "He was dressed in all white pearl beads going across, draped across," his sister LaToya told Barbara Walters. "A beautiful big gold belt. Like . . . a belt that you win being a boxer. Full makeup. . . . His hair was done beautifully, his makeup was done beautifully." He looked, said his sister, "absolutely fabulous."

✳ **THE MEMORIALS** Fans gathered everywhere, from the Jacksons' boyhood home in Gary, Ind. (above), to the Rock and Roll Hall of Fame and Museum in Cleveland (below). The L.A. memorial service (left) drew a TV audience of 31 million in the U.S. and a tender tribute from Jackson's daughter Paris, 11. "Ever since I was born, Daddy has been the best father you could ever imagine," she said. "I love him so much."

AU REVOIR
Parisian mourners produced an enormous Jackson banner.

JOHN *and* KATE
GOSSELIN
❋
May 25, 2009

Split Decision

On-camera and off, the bickering parents of eight go their separate ways

It began as a portrait of frazzled parenthood, light and airy as folded laundry. But this year it devolved into dark theater—the televised implosion of a family. The Gosselins of *Jon & Kate Plus 8*—a type-A mom and a whimpering dad raising twins and sextuplets—allowed their 10-year marriage to destruct in full view of tabs and TV cameras, starting with Jon's late-night jaunt with a 23-year-old female friend in April. The couple spoke of toughing it out as a new season of the TLC show began in May— "We're a family like anyone else, trying to survive," Jon told PEOPLE—but nothing could mask the tension between them: They even started shooting their cuddly "couch chats" separately. "He has a lot of anger," said Kate. "I have a lot of anger, too."

Then things got really nasty. Jon and Kate announced their breakup on the June 22 show, which drew more than 10 million viewers; that same day Kate filed for divorce. "Jon's activities have left me no choice," Kate declared, while Jon wasted no time jetting to France with Hailey Glassman, 22— the daughter of the plastic surgeon who performed Kate's tummy tuck. Communicating largely through lawyers and Larry King, the Gosselins kept up their scorched-earth split: She called police after he barred her from their Pennsylvania home; he went on *Good Morning America* and declared, "I despise [her]"; she accused him of draining a joint account of more than $200,000; he banned TLC cameras from filming the kids. The show, whittled down to *Kate Plus 8* in November, finally shut down—at least for now—while the couple continued negotiating their own cancelation. A tragic tale of reality TV gone wrong? That—and one of the year's saddest airings of dirty laundry.

JOHN TRAVOLTA
and KELLY PRESTON
✳
September 23, 2009

"Making him relive
that day is tough," a
friend said of Travolta
(with Preston, leaving
court in Nassau,
Bahamas, on Sept. 23).

FATHER AND SON
John "was just happy with anything that Jett offered," said a family friend. "Anything."

Losing Jett

John Travolta and Kelly Preston cope with the tragic loss of their son—and the dispiriting trial that followed

THE ACCUSED
Pleasant Bridgewater, a rising politician, and Tarino Lighbourn, a paramedic, were charged with trying to extort $25 million.

A family friend recalled the heartbreaking Jan. 2 phone call from Kelly Preston. "She said, 'There's been an accident,' and told me Jett was gone. I asked her if there was anything I could do, and she said, 'Just pray.'"

Jett Travolta, 16, John and Kelly's son, who was autistic, had suffered a severe seizure and, despite attempts by his father and medical personnel to revive him, was pronounced dead at Rand Memorial Hospital in Freeport, Bahamas, where the family owned a home. They were devastated. "Jett looked at John as if he was the sun and the moon," said Travolta's attorney Michael McDermott. "And John reciprocated." Said movie executive Sherry Lansing, another family friend: "John has the biggest heart in the whole world. I really can't imagine anything worse than this happening."

According to Travolta, something else did happen—not worse but still awful. The actor charged that two Bahamians—one a paramedic who had been at the scene—had tried to blackmail him for millions, claiming they could show he had been negligent in trying to save Jett. Despite the fact that one of the accused was caught on video acknowledging that he was committing "a criminal offense," the case was declared a mistrial—after a juror apparently leaked information about deliberations. Travolta and his attorney said they will seek a new trial.

BERNIE
MADOFF
✷
Arrested December 11, 2008

**MADOFF'S
MANY VICTIMS
INCLUDED:**

...KEVIN BACON and his
wife, Kyra Sedgwick

...STEVEN SPIELBERG and
mogul Jeffrey Katzenberg

**THE SWINDLER'S
WIFE**

Authorities tried
to recover assets from
RUTH MADOFF as well

Trust me

A mild-mannered charmer is judged "extraordinarily evil"

I'm responsible for a great deal of suffering and pain, I understand that," a seemingly contrite Bernie Madoff, whose $65 billion Ponzi scheme is thought to be the largest financial fraud in Wall Street history, said at his sentencing hearing in June. "I live in a tormented state now, knowing all of the pain and suffering that I've created."

Madoff's apparent remorse was of scant comfort to thousands of investors who entrusted the onetime lifeguard with their life savings. Among the victims of Madoff's massive swindle were large hedge funds, charities and philanthropic organizations, including the Elie Wiesel Foundation for Humanity and Steven Spielberg's Wunderkinder Foundation, as well as a multitude of small investors. "I was a millionaire," said one Arizona retiree, "and now I'm a pauper."

On June 29 a federal judge in New York City sentenced Madoff to 150 years in prison for his "extraordinarily evil crimes." On July 14 Madoff, who once enjoyed lavish homes in Manhattan, Montauk and Palm Beach, moved to a prison cell in North Carolina.

IN 1991
After Jaycee's disappearance, her mother "couldn't function."

People
JAYCEE DUGARD
KIDNAPPED 1991
DAVE'S DOUBLE LIFE NEW DETAILS
EXCLUSIVE PHOTOS
'I'M SO HAPPY TO BE BACK'
ONLY IN People The inside story of how the California kidnap survivor is loving life with her family and recovering from her 18-year ordeal

✳ J A Y C E E D U G A R D
August 26, 2009

IT WAS A MIRACLE, and a nightmare. In August police in Concord, Calif., discovered that Jaycee Dugard, 29, kidnapped 18 years ago, was alive and living with her alleged abductor, Phillip Garrido, 58. Another shock: Jaycee had two daughters, Angel, 15, and Starlit, 11, apparently fathered by Garrido, a registered sex offender. Jaycee and her daughters had never been to school or seen a doctor and seemed to have spent much of their lives in a cluster of windowless shacks in the backyard of Garrido's home outside Antioch, Calif., where he lived with his wife, Nancy, 54, and his ailing mother.

As for why Jaycee never tried to escape, "it's very difficult for any human being to be angry and desperate year after year,' said a kidnapping expert. "Jaycee figured out how to survive."

For that, her family is grateful. "I had given up hope," said her stepfather, Carl Probyn, 62. "To get her back after 18 years? I bawled for 10 minutes when I found out."

Jaycee and her daughters have been living with her mother, Terry Probyn, 50, and avoiding publicity. "They live a surprisingly normal life, considering the circumstances," says Terry's stepmother, Joan Curry. Said Jaycee: "I'm so happy to be back."

THE SUSPECT
Nancy and Phillip Garrido met while he was in prison for kidnapping a Reno casino worker in 1976. He allegedly kidnapped Jaycee three years after his release.

THE COMPOUND
The half-acre yard hid several tents and sheds.

Hero on the Hudson

*A cool, calm captain handles an in-flight nightmare
with finesse—and saves all his passengers in the process*

Ninety seconds after taking off from New York's LaGuardia Airport on Jan. 15, U.S. Airways Flight 1549 ran smack into an enormous flock of geese. Almost instantly, both of the Airbus's A320 engines died. "I knew the situation was bad immediately," said Capt. Chesley "Sully" Sullenberger III, 58. Yet, given his years of experience, he also knew that the stricken plane, and its passengers and crew, had a chance.

After calmly telling air-traffic controllers that he was unable to either return to LaGuardia or fly to a nearby airport in Teterboro, N.J., he quickly surmised that his only option was to bank left, aim over the George Washington Bridge and try to glide the plane to as smooth as possible a landing on the Hudson River. "I knew I could make a water landing," he said later.

Still, the experience was frightening. When Sullenberger announced, moments before the plane's belly hit the water, "Brace for impact!" flight attendant Doreen Welsh, 59, "was terrified for my soul," she said. She was in the rear of the plane, which quickly began filling with water after a passenger opened the tail door. At one point the water was up to her neck. "I was two seconds from drowning," she said. Thanks to Sullenberger's quick thinking, however, she and the 154 other passengers and crew survived the ordeal with no life-threatening injuries.

If it's possible to call a pilot uncommonly grounded, that certainly described Sullenberger.

Passenger Steve O'Brien recalls seeing the pilot sitting calmly in one of the life rafts. "He was so in control, I thought he was a rescuer," said O'Brien, 45. "He had a little clipboard, and he said, 'I need a count here of how many people.'"

Proving that even heroes are ultimately human, in the aftermath of the crash, Sullenberger, like many of his passengers and crew, was plagued by symptoms of post-traumatic stress. He had flashbacks and even wondered—incredibly—if he could have done anything better that day. "It's hard to shut your brain off," he said. "It's gotten much better, but at first I thought about the what-ifs." In the end, he's found comfort in returning to the skies, and in telling his story.

Sully Sullenberger still flies for U.S. Airways.

"IT TOOK A CREW OF FIVE TO ACCOMPLISH THIS, AND WE WERE DOING THE JOB WE WERE TRAINED FOR"

CAPTAIN
CHESLEY
SULLENBERGER III

February 8, 2009

✳ JILL PETERSON
and KEVIN HEINZ

June 20, 2009

BLUSHING BRIDE? Reluctant groom? Hardly. On June 20 Jill Peterson and Kevin Heinz literally danced down the aisle of Christ Lutheran Church in St. Paul to Chris Brown's R&B hit "Forever." Preceded by 16 boogying attendants, Heinz, 28, a law student, somer-saulted into the sanctuary. By the time psychology grad student Peterson, 29, clad in a silk Nicole Miller gown, gyrated toward her intended, guests were on their feet cheering. Says the groom's cousin Richelle Johnson: "I thought, 'Oh yeah, that's Kevin and Jill.'"

And then, via YouTube, the dance went viral, and the couple became insta-celebs. Credit for the dance idea goes to the bride, whose father suggested they post the result online. Said the groom: "[Jill's] dad had been really harassing me to kind of get it out to some of his other family members." And, by November 2009, to over 31 million viewers around the world.

✳ **VIRAL VIDEO** The duo's fame "wasn't expected," said Kevin's uncle. "But it's nice to know people share common things like music and dancing."

Wild Ride

One night, one song, and instant stardom

Normally when Susan Boyle, 48, visits her local pub in sleepy Blackburn, Scotland, she sits at a table alone, sips from her soda and, if it's karaoke night, belts out a few show tunes. But on April 12—the day after she stunned the world with her soaring rendition of "I Dreamed a Dream" on *Britain's Got Talent*—the scene at the pub was much less subdued. Boyle entered the bar, and "it was chaos," says manager Jackie Russell. "There was a standing ovation. Her face went beet-red."

Chalk it up to a weary world eager for uplifting entertainment, the surprise of a diamond-in-the-rough performer or simply the delight of watching *BGT* judge and resident grinch Simon Cowell grow a heart right before the audience's eyes. But clearly the self-described "short and plump" Boyle—whose performance has scored more than 70 million YouTube views—struck a chord. "I'm taking it all in my stride," she told PEOPLE in early May.

That stride broke a month later when, after losing the *BGT* title to dance troupe Diversity, Boyle, exhausted, landed in a North London hospital. "She had a really tough time dealing with [it all]," says *BGT*'s Piers Morgan of the speed with which the shy Scottish singer rocketed to fame.

By September she was happily recovered, jetting across the ocean to make her U.S. debut. As for the now-infamous matter of her never-been-kissed status? "No comment," says Boyle.

SUSAN
BOYLE
✳
May 30, 2009

BALLOON
BOY
✳
October 15, 2009

Look! Up in the Sky! It's a Hoax!

Coloradan Richard Heene reported a silvery balloon he had built had escaped its tether and that his son, Falcon, age 6, might be aboard. Fearing the worst, authorities tracked the craft, and breathless cable news anchors kept a mesmerized public updated. Finally, the balloon landed—without Falcon! But wait ... could it be? Yes! A miracle! He had been hiding in an attic all along! Cheers! Hugs! National

rejoicing! And ... cut!

The only problem? It was all a scam, cooked up by Heene, 48, who apparently hoped to create interest in a reality-TV show he was marketing. (Falcon innocently helped reveal the fraud when he blurted, on *Larry King Live,* "Um, we did this for the show.")

Humiliated, Heene and his wife, Mayumi, 45, pleaded guilty to various charges, and were due to be sentenced in December.

SPACE CASE
Richard Heene and son Falcon
(top); below, the shiny object
that mesmerized millions.

✳ NADYA SULEMAN

January 26, 2009

ALTHOUGH THE GOSSELINS certainly deserve an honorable mention, the 2009 Modern Media Perfect Storm and Possible Sign of the Approaching Apocalypse Award should probably go to Octomom, whose one-of-a-kind media moniker—which she later copyrighted—pretty much says it all.

On Jan. 26 Nadya Suleman, 34, gave birth to octuplets and made headlines. And, very quickly, ignited controversy. Unmarried, unemployed and living with her parents, Suleman already had six children under the age of 8 before reportedly having herself implanted with multiple embryos. Immediately, the media erupted with commentary about her decision to have more—especially when it was revealed that she was already receiving food stamps for her other children.

Then—metaphorically speaking—the circus came to town. On *The Dr. Phil Show*, one of a group of volunteer nannies who had helped care for the newborns, and then was fired, accused Suleman of lousy parenting. "This woman does not care for these kids," said Linda West-Conforit. "She is in [it] for the paparazzi, the media. . . . Nadya only fed the babies [herself] . . . when a film crew was in her house." (Suleman denied the charges.) Her fertility doctor, Dr. Michael Kamrava, was drummed out of the American Society of Reproductive Medicine. Activist attorney Gloria Allred, alleging that Sulemen spent much of her time shopping, campaigned to have the octuplets put into foster care. On the commercial side of the equation, Suleman's lawyer sought to trademark the name "Octomom"; an Octomom musical opened in L.A.; and she signed a deal for a reality-TV show.

Judging from appearances, the hubbub didn't upset Suleman: On Halloween, she dressed the octuplets as devils and herself as a pregnant nun.

> "SHE'S A GOOD MOTHER. SHE HAS TO LEARN TO TAKE CARE OF HER CHILDREN"
> —NADYA'S MOTHER, ANGELA

IN THE ROUGH
A humbled Woods (with Elin in 2002) promised, "I will strive to be a better person and the husband and father my family deserves."

✳ TIGER TROUBLE

THE FIRST PEOPLE ON THE SCENE could hardly believe their eyes—Tiger Woods, the world's top golfer, was lying in the street at 2:30 a.m. "His eyes rolled back into his head and he lost consciousness," says one onlooker. "I thought he could be paralyzed or die."

Woods was, physically, okay—he'd driven his Cadillac Escalade into a tree outside his home in Windermere, Fla., and was released from a hospital within hours—but in the ensuing days his public image would take a beating. Just before his Nov. 27 crash, the *National Enquirer* reported that Woods was having an affair with nightclub hostess Rachel Uchitel (who denied it); rumors immediately began swirling that the golfing great had been leaving his house at that hour—and, apparently, at a good rate of speed—after a domestic row with his wife, Elin, 29.

On Nov. 29 Woods issued a statement admitting he was "not perfect," while simultaneously decrying "false, unfounded and malicious rumors" and asking for privacy. Three days later, as more claims of possible marital infidelity surfaced, he addressed the rumors more directly: "I have let my family down, and I regret those transgressions with all of my heart," he said. "I have not been true to my values and the behavior my family deserves. . . . I am dealing with my behavior and personal failings behind closed doors with my family. . . . For all those who have supported me over the years, I offer my profound apology."

SARAH PALIN

July 26, 2009

Rogue in Vogue

The would-be Veep takes defeat standing up

"AS EVERY IDITAROD MUSHER KNOWS: IF YOU'RE NOT THE LEAD DOG, THE VIEW NEVER CHANGES"

—SARAH PALIN

After the licking she and her ticket mate John McCain took the previous November, former Republican vice-presidential candidate Sarah Palin might easily have retired from the national scene, resumed her duties as governor of the 49th state and continued to give moose everywhere field-dressing nightmares.

Palin, however, seemed to want more—and on her terms. Surprising virtually everyone, she resigned her governorship a year before her term ended, lay low (while communing with the faithful via Twitter and giving speeches at which no reporters were allowed) and wrote an instant, and controversial, bestseller, *Going Rogue: An American Life*, in which she told her life story and settled scores with McCain campaign workers who, she maintained, had misled, misrepresented and misused her.

As for any possible plans to run for President in 2012, Palin said she was flattered, but unmoved, by crowds shouting "Run! Sarah! Run!" during her book tour. Then again, as she wrote in *Going Rogue,* "As every Iditarod musher knows: If you're not the lead dog, the view never changes."

SONIA
SOTOMAYOR
August 12, 2009

History on the Bench

A Bronx-born Yankees fan becomes the Supreme Court's first Latina justice

Sonia Sotomayor learned a lot growing up in a South Bronx housing project. Among other things, recalled her brother Juan, now a doctor, "we learned never to let anyone walk behind you." Also, there was more than one way to handle a difficult situation. "If I had a kid picking on me, she would try to negotiate," said Juan. "If she couldn't, she would move on to step two. She could mix it up."

Conflict resolution at her new job may be just as energetic if, in all likelihood, far less physical: On Aug. 8, 2009, Sotomayor, 55, was sworn in as the newest member of the U.S. Supreme Court. While compiling a résumé that includes 17 years as a federal judge and five years in the office of the New York City prosecutor,

Sotomayor earned a reputation as "tough on people and intellectually rigorous, and we want that in our judges," said her Yale Law classmate Rudolph Aragon.

She is also anything but an ivory-tower type. Her father was a factory worker and her mother a nurse; they skimped elsewhere to provide for their children's education and books. After her father died suddenly when she was 9, Sotomayor found solace in reading and studied her way to Princeton, followed by Yale Law.

Despite all the hard work, Sotomayor, who is divorced, knows how to relax. Every Christmas she goes a little nuts decorating her Manhattan apartment, and, for her 50th birthday, she took salsa lessons, then threw a party to show off her steps.

✳ CAPTAIN RICHIE PHILLIPS
April 17, 2009

AS FOUR ARMED SOMALI pirates climbed aboard the U.S.-flagged cargo ship *Maersk Alabama* early on April 8, most of the 19 crewmen followed procedure and locked themselves below deck. Burly skipper Richie Phillips, however, stayed on the bridge. And when a pirate demanded he summon the crew, he made the announcement—but did not use the prearranged code word that would have signalled crewmen that it was safe to come out. "He thought on his feet," said third engineer John Cronin. "He let us know it would be best to remain in place."

Those crewmen emerged unscathed, but the saga only grew deadlier for Phillips, 54. The Somalis held him hostage in a lifeboat for five days   his one escape attempt was thwarted by the pirates—until Navy SEAL snipers aboard a U.S. warship dramatically shot the Somalis and rescued him on April 12. Five days later Phillips finally landed on U.S. soil, where the Vermonter was greeted at Burlington International Airport by his wife, Andrea, 52, and their children Mariah, 19, and Daniel, 20. Well-wishers hoisted signs and American flags, and many more waited on front porches and tree-lined streets to cheer as state troopers escorted the family back to their modest white farmhouse.

"I am just a bit part in this story," he said at the airport. "I am not the hero. The military is the hero." The *Alabama* crewmen who spoke with PEOPLE tell a different story. As third mate Colin Wright gratefully explained, "It is because of his professionalism that we made it out of there."

IN CUSTODY In late April, Abduhl Wali-i-Musi, the only surviving Somali pirate, arrived at the federal courthouse in New York City, where he was arraigned on piracy charges.

HOME AT LAST After his rescue (top, with Commander Frank Castellano on the USS *Bainbridge*), Phillips reunited with his children Mariah and Daniel in Vermont and enjoyed a meal of true comfort food: chicken potpie and his mother-in-law's brownies.

JESSICA
SIMPSON
✴

Animals

*Cloned dogs, and pooches lost and
found, made news in 2009*

Jessica's Pet Tragedy

At 8:13 on the night of Sept. 14, Jessica Simpson, 29, tweeted that her dog, a maltipoo she'd owned for five years, had been taken by a coyote as she watched in Los Angeles. "My heart is broken because a coyote took my precious Daisy right in front of our eyes. HORROR!" she tweeted. "We are searching. Hoping. Please help!" Fans remained glued to their Twitter feeds. By Wednesday, a dog-finding service, FindToto.com, had made calls to some 1,000 of her neighbors asking if they'd spotted any sign of Daisy. Alas, the missing maltipoo was never recovered.

Missing
Malti-Poo
Caramel Colored
REWARD
OFFERED
Email info to: www.
FINDINGMISSDAISY@GMAIL.COM

I miss my mommy . "Daisy"

DOG GONE, NOW BACK
Sophie (reunited with owner Jan Griffith, above) swam five miles and lived for four months on St. Bees island (left).

☀ THE INCREDIBLE JOURNEY OF A CANINE CRUSOE

IN NOVEMBER 2008, Jan and David Griffith hit rough seas during a day trip along the Great Barrier Reef. Struggling at the wheel of their 34-ft. motorboat, they didn't see their Australian cattle dog, Sophie Tucker, 4, fall overboard. "We took our eyes off her for a moment, and she was gone," says Jan. They searched that day and the next before returning to their Mackay, Queensland, home, devastated. They were certain they'd seen the last of the house pet who, says Jan, "was so much part of our lives." Little did they know that after Sophie hit the water, she swam more than five miles to the largely deserted St. Bees island and survived for four months by catching her own food—until she was discovered by rangers during a routine check. "What she did was extraordinary," says animal behaviorist Teka Ludovico. "Eating kibble to hunting is a huge adjustment."

LANCELOT: THE NEXT GENERATION
The Ottos with a favorite photo, and a very furry photocopy.

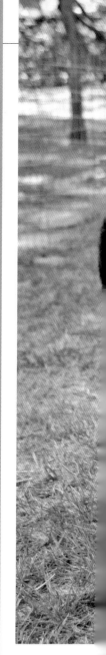

✸ FOR $155,000, A CUTE LAB FROM THE LAB

WHEN EDGAR AND NINA OTTO lost their Labrador retriever, Lancelot, to cancer in 2008, they still had plenty of wildlife on their 12-acre Florida spread: four birds, 10 cats, six sheep and nine pooches (Edgar's father was a cofounder of NASCAR; he himself founded a successful medical company). But they missed their top dog. So when they heard that BioArts International, a California biotech firm, was holding a "dog-cloning auction," they shelled out a whopping $155,000 and won the right to have Lancelot cloned (they'd frozen some of his DNA six years before). The result? Lancelot Encore, the first made-to-order single cloned pup, who "bonded immediately, within an hour, with every other pet in the house," said Nina.

FIVE OF A KIND
Symington at Ground Zero with Trakr in 2001 (below) and, right, with a quintet of clones who, he says, match Trakr's appearance "down to the smallest detail."

A 9/11 Hero's Hi-Tech Return

Trakr, the German shepherd credited with finding the last survivor in the smoking rubble of 9/11's Ground Zero, died in April—but that's not the last his owner has seen of him. James Symington, a retired Canadian police officer, entered an essay contest, won the opportunity to have Trackr cloned and took home five new Trakrs ("They're identical," he says) in June. "Few dogs are born with exceptional abilities—Trakr was one of those dogs," says Symington, who adds that if these copies have the same abilities as the original, he intends to put them to work as search-and-rescue dogs.

NON-IRONIC
Letterman admitted his misbehavior and went after his alleged blackmailer.

Don't Mess with Dave

TV had never seen anything like it. On the Oct. 1 *Late Show,* David Letterman looked into the camera, told his audience he had slept with women on his staff, said someone had used that information to try to blackmail him for $2 million and announced police had arrested a suspect. Then came another shock: The suspect was a respected CBS news producer, Robert "Joe" Halderman, 52. He pleaded not guilty.

Details about the love life of the intensely private talk show host began to emerge. No staffer accused Letterman, 62, of unwanted advances, but his romantic world was, indeed, messy. According to sources, Letterman had at one point dated an employee, Stephanie Birkitt, now 35, who later dated Halderman—and, according to court papers in the case, continued to see the talk show host. Letterman had also been dating Regina Lasko, 48, for more than 20 years; they had a child in 2003 and married in 2009. Letterman alleged that Halderman had wanted to sell a screenplay about the host's life and had threatened that "[Letterman's] world was about to collapse around him"—unless he paid up.

Four days later Letterman again addressed his audience, to say he was "terribly sorry" and that his wife had been "horribly hurt by my behavior, and when something happens like that . . . you try to fix it . . . so let me tell you folks: I got my work cut out for me."

CHRIS BROWN *and* RIHANNA
✦

Law

Chris Brown, David Letter and the trial of an American student in Italy make headlines

> "I AM TRULY SORRY THAT I WASN'T ABLE TO HANDLE THE SITUATION"

NEARLY A YEAR LATER, the story still shocks: On Feb. 8, hours after they had been photographed staring dreamily at each other, Chris Brown and Rihanna got into a fight that left the pretty pop star bruised and bloodied. The next day the formerly squeaky-clean R&B singer surrendered to the L.A. police. According to a police affidavit, the argument was sparked by a text message Brown, now 20, received from a former flame; as tempers flared, he bit, choked and punched Rihanna, now 21. "I have told Rihanna countless times, and I am telling you today," Brown said in a statement in July, "that I am truly sorry that I wasn't able to handle the situation both differently and better."

In June Brown pleaded guilty to felony assault and was later sentenced to five years probation, six months of community labor and a year of domestic violence classes. He accepted his punishment ("The law is the law") and vowed to learn. "I want to understand my feelings… this has matured me," he said. But one part of his sentence caught him off-guard: He was ordered not to contact Rihanna for five years. Said Brown: "I couldn't say goodbye."

&order

HOURS BEFORE
Rihanna and Brown had attended a pre-Grammy party (above) earlier that night.

THE WRECKAGE "Being a mother was everything to her." said a friend. "None of what is going on makes sense."

✳ KIEFER SUTHERLAND *and* JACK McCOLLOUGH

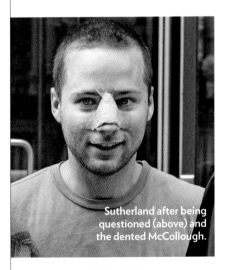

Sutherland after being questioned (above) and the dented McCollough.

"THE COMPLAINING WITNESS . . . WAS QUITE UNCOOPERATIVE"
—A MANHATTAN D.A. SPOKESWOMAN

AT A NIGHTCLUB IN May, *24* actor Kiefer Sutherland head-butted a guy who bumped into Brooke Shields. The buttee—fashion designer Jack McCollough, 31, whom Shields later said had *not* been bothering her—wound up with a broken nose.

Though initially charged with third-degree assault, Sutherland, 43, privately resolved his differences with McCollough, who then accepted a public apology from the actor, wished him well—and decided to say nothing more, even to the police. Not surprisingly, the case then evaporated.

"We declined to prosecute after a full investigation," said Manhattan District Attorney spokeswoman Alicia Maxey Greene. "That included speaking to the complaining witness, who was quite uncooperative."

The Schulers on their wedding day, and (below) with Bryan, who survived, and Erin.

Wrong Way, at 80 mph

A mom's deadly drive leaves behind grief, anger and a mystery

It made no sense. Months later it still doesn't.

On July 26 Diane Schuler, with five kids packed into her brother's minivan, turned the wrong way onto the Taconic State Parkway in Westchester County, N.Y., and sped for nearly two miles into oncoming traffic. "For a minute we were like, 'Is that a car?'" recalled Corey Lowe, an eyewitness. "It came speeding past us at like 80 mph. It was the eeriest thing I ever saw." Seconds later Schuler ran head-on into an SUV, and eight people were dead: Schuler, 36; her daughter Erin, 2; her nieces Emma, 8, Alyson, 7, and Kate, 5; and Michael Bastardi, 81, his son Guy, 49, and their friend Daniel Longo, 74, who were in the SUV. Schuler's son Bryan, 5, survived.

Her husband, Daniel, 38, and friends in her town of West Babylon, N.Y., reeled with grief—and then came another blow. Toxicology tests showed Schuler had twice the legal limit of alcohol in her blood and had smoked marijuana shortly before the accident. "This is so out of the realm of possibility, it just blows my mind," said Christine Lipani, 47, who, like many of Schuler's friends, insisted that the Diane they knew—devoted parent, virtual teetotaler—could never do something so reckless. "She was not an alcoholic," Daniel said of his wife of seven years. "I never saw her drunk since the day I met her." Daniel suggested that some other, undetected medical issue may have sparked her behavior.

Months later the big question—why was an outwardly typical suburban mom, with a vehicle full of kids, speeding down the wrong side of a highway?—remains unanswered.

Murder in Italy

American Amanda Knox, in Perugia, Italy, for her junior year, stands trial for a grisly killing

The crime was sensational; ditto the headlines. In 2007 British college student Meredith Kercher, 21, was found in her bedroom in Perugia with her throat slit. Portraying her death as the result of a sadomasochistic sex game gone awry, police accused University of Washington student Knox, now 22, her then-boyfriend, Italian Raffaele Sollecito, 25, and Ivorian Rudy Guede, 22, of murder. The Italian and British press portrayed Knox as an "angel-faced killer"; according to her parents and friends, she is an innocent, uncommonly sweet girl being railroaded by a rabid prosecutor.

At Knox's trial, several of Kercher's friends described what they considered Knox's bizarre behavior when she was brought into the police station for questioning the day after the murder. Knox blithely began doing cartwheels and handstands and snuggling with Sollecito. "We were

all crying, and I didn't see Amanda crying," said Robyn Butterworth. "She and Raffaele were kissing and joking." On the stand, Knox explained, "When I feel uneasy or nervous, I act a bit foolish."

Knox, who, investigators say, initially gave them contradictory information about where she had been the night of the murder, also testified that she had been slapped by police and coerced into making incriminating statements. "They were putting me under extreme amounts of pressure," she said. "I was confused." A knife that may or may not have been the murder weapon had her DNA on the handle and the victim's on the blade, but defense attorneys insisted it could be innocently explained.

Guede, who was tried separately, was convicted of murder in October and sentenced to 30 years. As this book was going to press, Knox's fate was far from certain; a verdict was due in December 2009.

> # "THEY WERE PUTTING ME UNDER EXTREME AMOUNTS OF PRESSURE. I WAS CONFUSED"

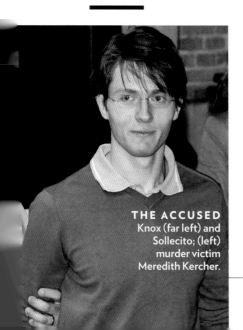

THE ACCUSED
Knox (far left) and Sollecito; (left) murder victim Meredith Kercher.

✳ BYRD *and* MELANIE BILLINGS

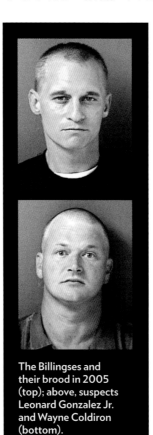

The Billingses and their brood in 2005 (top); above, suspects Leonard Gonzalez Jr. and Wayne Coldiron (bottom).

ON JULY 9, INTRUDERS burst into the home of Byrd and Melanie Billings and shot them to death. The couple had 16 children, 12 of them adopted, many with special needs. "I just wanted to give them a better life," Melanie once explained.

Police quickly arrested seven suspects, identified through a surveillance system that Byrd, 66, and Melanie, 43, had rigged around their home near Pensacola, Fla., to ensure their kids' safety. Sheriff David Morgan said the intruders were bent on robbery. But he also hinted at further twists, saying authorities were looking for additional accomplices and that other motives were likely to emerge.

Ashley Markham, 27, Melanie's daughter from an earlier marriage, said the family would remain together and that the grown children would continue her parents' work. "Mom and Dad only had love in their lives," she said. "They had a calling . . . to provide love to children that most did not see as normal. . . . Mom and Dad will give us the strength to make it through."

ALYSSA MILANO
and DAVID BUGLIARI

August 15, 2009

Weddings

Movie stars, small-screen celebrities and two tennis sensations choose 2009 as the year to say "I do"

STAGE FRIGHT
"Having everyone's eyes on me made me nervous!" said the bride.

The ring pillow was a bird's nest, the cocktail tables were hay bales, and the aisles were grass, strewn with petals. "Every detail was a reflection of our love for family and nature," said actress Alyssa Milano, 36, of her wedding to Hollywood agent David Bugliari, 30. "We wanted a laid-back event with a relaxed feel."

The traditional ceremony, held at the New Jersey estate of her new husband's family, was performed by an Episcopalian priest and included a reading by actor Bradley Cooper, a friend and client of the groom's. Afterward the newlyweds and their 175 guests headed for a nearby tent and danced until 2:30. "They were radiant as light bulbs, with smiles wrapped around their faces," said event planner Colin Cowie. "I predict they'll be together forever."

LISA LOEB *and*
ROEY HERSHKOVITZ
✳
January 31, 2009

✳ MANDY MOORE and RYAN ADAMS
March 10, 2009

SHOW BIZ? SCHMO BIZ. All Mandy Moore and Ryan Adams needed for their perfect wedding was a tiny brick church, a pastor they had just met, a pair of silver bands and each other.

"She was thrilled to be getting married," said Pastor Steve Schulte, who married the couple at Whitefield Chapel at Bethesda Home for Boys on the outskirts of Savannah, Ga. "She was giddy but not in a childish way. She was obviously so happy."

The couple dressed down: Moore, 24, wore a cream-colored, lacy tea-length dress and flat sandals; Adams, 34, had on skinny jeans, a T-shirt, a sport coat and sneakers. After an eight-minute ceremony, Schulte said, "I now pronounce you husband and wife," and the couple kissed, smiled and walked out.

"It was so romantic—it was awesome," said Chad Baker, a friend of Schulte's who saw the couple. "I just can't stress how happy they seemed."

I was thinking, 'Maybe I should've rehearsed this,'" Lisa Loeb recalled of nervously walking down the aisle, in a light pink gown and 3½" heels, as her wedding began. "It was one time where I was winging it, but I wanted to be in the moment."

During the ceremony Loeb, 40, and *Late Night with Conan O'Brien* music supervisor Roey Hershkovitz, 30, "took turns laughing and crying," said the groom. For the reception, Loeb dreamed up an all-white winter wonderland complete with deer figurines and "custom-made Muppets that looked like us that guests danced with."

At an afterparty, the newlyweds and their guests played the video game Rock Band until 4 a.m. "We were exhausted," said Loeb, "but it was the most fun night ever!"

HEIDI MONTAG
and SPENCER PRATT
✹
April 25, 2009

Once more, with feeling, and sky-writing: After an impromptu Mexican wedding in November 2008—which did not include family or friends—Heidi Montag, 22, and Spencer Pratt, 25, love-to-hate-'em stars of *The Hills*, exchanged vows again on April 25 before 200 guests, including costars Audrina Patridge, Brody Jenner and Lauren Conrad, at Westminster Presbyterian Church in Pasadena, Calif.

The couple arrived in a white Rolls Royce Phantom; before the ceremony, a plane flew over and wrote "Spencer loves Heidi" in the sky. The bride, who wore a Monique Lhuillier gown and more than $1 million in Neil Lane jewelry, tweeted throughout her big day, at one point tapping out, "Thank you God for Spencer."

HONEYMOON
The duo evaded the swine flu in Cabo, Mexico.

JUST DESSERTS
The cake matched the bridesmaids' yellow dresses.

GISELE BUNDCHEN *and* TOM BRADY

April 4, 2009

For supermodel Gisele Bündchen, 28, and quarterback Tom Brady, 31, as the year began, there was a whole lotta romance going on.

The couple became engaged in January, tied the knot weeks later in a top-secret ceremony in Santa Monica, then, in April, staged a more glamorous second wedding at Bündchen's home in the seaside village of Santa Teresa, Costa Rica. The three-day affair began with dinner and cocktails at a local hotel, followed the next day by a barbecue (Gisele wore a bikini). On the big night, Bündchen covered her patio with white and yellow orchids and calla lilies. As Brady's trainer, Oscar Smith, put it after wedding No. 1, "He is a superathlete, and she is a supermodel. They belong together."

✳ M I L L A   J O V O V I C H
and P A U L   W . S .   A N D E R S O N

August 22, 2009

JOVOVICH AND ANDERSON, 47, first met in 2002, when he directed her in the box office hit *Resident Evil*. In 2007 they had a daughter, Ever Gabo. This year they felt the time was right to get hitched, with a touch of Latin style (before the ceremony at their Beverly Hills home, a Spanish guitarist played for guests; afterward the reception included music by Cuban drummers).

The future, they hope, will include more children, pretty much ASAP. "Having a child has completely changed the way I look at my life," Jovovich, 34, told PEOPLE earlier in the year. "I don't worry about my career or what other people think about me. My main priority now is my child and my family. . . . I don't know what the future will hold, but knock on wood, I hope it'll bring me a big family."

✱ **BRUCE WILLIS**
and **EMMA HEMING**
March 21, 2009

"**UNLESS THE HAND** of God intervenes," Bruce Willis told PEOPLE in 2005, "I'm going to go out as a bachelor."

Divine intervention came in the form of British model Emma Heming, 32, whom he met a few years ago. After their first date, Willis, 54, told *W* magazine, "I went from 'F--- love' to 'Love is truly the answer.'" After splitting from Demi Moore in 1998, said Willis, "I spent the last 10 years single and, for the most part, unhappy. . . . I would say, 'I'm alone, but I'm not lonely.' But I was just kidding myself. Then I started hanging around Emma, and on a day-to-day basis, my life became much happier."

Willis and Heming exchanged vows twice: on March 21 on Parrot Cay in Turks and Caicos, with his daughters (Rumer, 20, Scout, 17, and Tallulah, 15), ex-wife Moore and her husband, Ashton Kutcher, in attendance; and a week later at a civil ceremony in Beverly Hills. Says Willis: "She's not only my best friend, but my wife."

✱ **DAVID LETTERMAN**
and **REGINA LASKO**
March 19, 2009

THERE WOULD BE HEADLINES later (see page 37), but the marriage of talk show host David Letterman and longtime girlfriend Regina Lasko could not have been more subdued. "Seeing David was a surprise," said Lisa Sinton, Clerk of District Court in Teton County, Mont. "They used a friend to call in to get the information about what they needed to do, so I really had no idea it was going to be David."

The bride wore a navy blue suit. The groom was dressed neatly, despite the fact that his truck had gotten stuck in the mud on the way to the ceremony.

After Sinton issued the license, Letterman, 61, and Lasko, 48—with their 5-year-old son Harry in tow— went upstairs to justice of the peace Pete Howard, who officiated. Genevieve and Lee Barhaugh, friends of the couple, witnessed the ceremony.

Back on the show, Letterman, typically enigmatic about his private life, quipped, "People say, 'Jeez, Dave, you were together so long. Does it feel any different?' And I say, 'Yeah. It does.'"

ALI LARTER *and* HAYES MacARTHUR

August 1, 2009

Carrying a simple bouquet of blush-pink roses, *Heroes* actress Ali Larter, 33, married her longtime beau, actor Hayes MacArthur, 32, at his parents' estate in Kennebunkport, Maine, on Aug. 1. Larter, in a Vera Wang gown, walked down a grassy aisle lined with rose petals before exchanging vows under a canopy of trees. "[He] brought light to my life," Larter has said about her husband. "I feel lucky every morning when I wake up and see him."

SALMA HAYEK
and FRANCOIS-HENRI
PINAULT
✳
April 25, 2009

"IT WAS ALL ABOUT LOVE, FAMILY AND FRIENDS"
—A WEDDING GUEST

Venice's Teatro La Fenice was filled with music—but far less Verdi than usual. During Salma Hayek's wedding to French luxury-goods mogul François-Henri Pinault, Edward Norton and Woody Harrelson led 150 guests—including Penélope Cruz, Charlize Theron and Ashley Judd—in a rendition of "Over the Rainbow." Later, Bono joined the bride for a performance of "Stand by Me." Said a guest of the wedding weekend, which began with a carnival-style masked ball: "It was one magical moment after another."

Hayek, 42, and Pinault, 46, who have a 19-month-old daughter, Valentina, had already wed once, in a small civil ceremony in Paris on Valentine's Day. For round 2, they recited their own vows. Later, at an elegant reception, guests enjoyed a dinner prepared by top chef José Andrés before hitting the dance floor to a 14-piece band. For their first dance, the couple chose Bruce Springsteen's "Drive All Night." Said a guest: "It was a night to remember."

✱ FERGIE *and* JOSH DUHAMEL
January 10, 2009

THE BLACK EYED PEA wore white—not surprising, given that Fergie, 33, was marrying her beau of four years, *Las Vegas* star Josh Duhamel, 36, in a glamorous setting before about 350 guests, including the rest of Fergie's Pea pod; Rebecca Romijn and Jerry O'Connell; Mario Lopez; Kid Rock; Slash; Wilmer Valderrama; James Caan; and Duhamel's family, who flew in from his home state, North Dakota. "They're so excited," said a friend. "They really love Fergie and are so happy to welcome her to the family." Actor Mario Lopez—who at age 10 shared his first kiss with Fergie, then known as Stacy Ferguson and his costar on *Kids Incorporated*—seemed to have got over any lingering jealousy. "Josh," he said, "is a great guy. They will be great together."

After the ceremony, guests adjourned to a tent and—thanks to a small miracle of decoration—danced in an enchanted forest.

IVANKA TRUMP
and JARED KUSHNER

✳

October 25, 2009

Ivanka Trump wore a custom Vera Wang gown inspired by Grace Kelly when she wed Jared Kushner, 28, publisher of the *New York Observer,* in front of more than 500 guests at the Trump National Golf Club in Bedminster, N.J. The megawatt crowd included stars Russell Crowe, Natalie Portman and Regis Philbin.

"They're really a beautiful, smart couple," Donald Trump, father of the bride—and her *Celebrity Apprentice* costar—said of the newly-weds. "I think you'll hear a lot of great things from them in the years to come."

✴ ROGER FEDERER
and MIRKA VAVRINEC
April 11, 2009

HE'S ONE OF THE GREATEST singles players in tennis history, but this year Roger Federer, 27, made news for doubles—twice. In April he married his longtime girlfriend Miroslava "Mirka" Vavrinec, 31, in an intimate ceremony in his hometown of Basel, Switzerland. "It was a beautiful spring day and an incredibly joyous occasion," Federer wrote on his blog. "Mr. and Mrs. Roger Federer wish all of you a happy Easter weekend."

In July, Mirka, a former professional tennis player, gave birth to twin girls, Myla and Charlene. Within hours, a British betting house was offering 200-1 odds that the twins would one day win the women's doubles title at Wimbledon.

✴ ANDY RODDICK
and BROOKLYN DECKER
April 17, 2009

A RAINSTORM BLOCKED out the sunset but didn't dampen the mood. "They were so excited," said an attendee at the Texas wedding of swimsuit model Brooklyn Decker and tennis star Andy Roddick, 26. "They had looked forward to this for so long."

After the couple exchanged Tiffany rings, the party moved from a tent outside Roddick's Austin home to the nearby Westwood Country Club, where Sir Elton John—who knows Roddick through mutual charity work—performed a 10-song set. "They were all of Andy and Brooklyn's favorites," said a friend. "It was something they'll remember their entire lives."

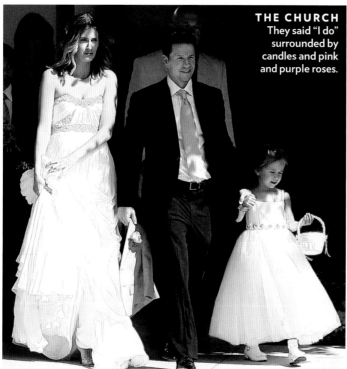

THE CHURCH
They said "I do" surrounded by candles and pink and purple roses.

✳ M A R K   W A H L B E R G
and R H E A   D U R H A M
August 1, 2009

IT TOOK ABOUT 10 YEARS and three kids, but on Aug. 1, Mark Wahlberg, 38, wed model Rhea Durham, 31, at the Good Shepherd Catholic Church in Beverly Hills. About a dozen guests and children Brendan, 11 months, Michael, 3, and Ella, 5 (who did flower-girl duty in a dress that matched her mom's Marchesa gown), attended. How do Wahlberg and Durham feel about making it official? On the way to a pink-and-white reception at their L.A. home, said a source, "they looked so happy; they kept kissing the whole way."

SHANIA TWAIN *and*
FREDERIC THIEBAUD

November 18, 2008

THE TWAIN MEET
"Fred and I," Shania
wrote, "have certainly
had a lot of laughs."

Country superstar Shania Twain's marriage to producer Robert "Mutt" Lange, 61, exploded spectacularly in May 2008, when she discovered that he had been having an affair with her best friend, Marie-Anne Thiébaud, 39, a longtime secretary and manager of the couple's château in Switzerland.

A little more than a year later, Twain, 44, posted a nearly 15-minute video travelogue on her Web site showing fans what she had been doing (skydiving, riding camels in Egypt) and—while neither saying nor denying that the relationship was romantic—singing the joys of having a particular "dear friend and true gentleman" in her life. His identity was both surprising and not: Marie-Anne's ex-husband, Frédéric Thiébaud, 39.

"Having gone through the suffering of his family splitting apart at the same time and under the same extreme circumstances, he understands me better than anyone," Twain wrote. "We leaned on one another through the ups and downs, taking turns holding each other up. We've become stronger and closer through it all, as have our children [her 8-year-old son] Eja and Johanna, Fred's 8-year-old daughter."

Close enough, and happy enough, that a friend, said the unwaveringly coy Twain, "refers to us as Lucy and Ricky Ricardo."

Babies

A young Sparrow (Nicole and Joel's second), a boy cub for Tiger and another Duggar (that's 18!) made their debuts

SARAH JESSICA PARKER
and
MATTHEW BRODERICK

**Marion Loretta Elwell
and Tabitha Hodge,
June 22, 2009, 5 lbs. 11 oz. and 6 lbs.**

Sarah Jessica Parker and Matthew Broderick's son James Wilkie, 7, was "pretty excited," his dad said, at the news he'd soon have two sisters: "He said, 'We have to get a lot of princess toys.'" The twin princesses, Marion Loretta Elwell and Tabitha Hodge (Hodge and Elwell are family names on Parker's side), were born to a surrogate and arrived in June. "They love kids and wanted more," said a family friend. "They absolutely love being parents." Parker, 44, expressed her deep gratitude, saying the surrogate made an "incredibly generous and gracious choice."

BRISTOL PALIN
and
LEVI JOHNSTON

✳

Tripp, December 27, 2008,
7 lbs. 4 oz.

HER NEW
TRIPP
"I know I can't
do this by
myself," said
Bristol. "I'm
thankful for my
huge family."

In her 18th year Bristol Palin helped her mom run for vice president, graduated from high school, had a baby and broke up with the baby's father, Levi Johnston, 19. It was a full year. And though she dearly loves her son Tripp, born Dec. 27, 2008, she's quick to caution other teenagers to think very hard before risking pregnancy. "Girls need to imagine and picture their life with a screaming newborn baby," she said, "and then think before they have sex."

"I NEVER IN A TRILLION YEARS WOULD HAVE THOUGHT IT WOULD HAPPEN TO ME"

Her own life changed abruptly. Although she finished high school—returning five days after Tripp's birth—she went to class sleep-deprived, then rushed home to feed her son. She quit sports, rarely saw friends and tapped out at least one paper with Tripp crying in the background. She skipped prom and worked $10-an-hour babysitting jobs to help pay for Tripp's needs and put less of a burden on her parents. "It makes you mature a ton," Bristol said. "My life comes second now." She loves her boy, but clearly wishes she had waited until she was ready. "If girls realized the consequences of sex, nobody would be having sex," said Bristol. "Trust me. Nobody."

HELLO HOLDEN! The newcomer joined Johnny (left), Mattea and Mom and Dad.

✴ MIRA SORVINO and CHRISTOPHER BACKUS
Holden, June 22, 2009, 8 lbs. 12 oz.

"AS SOON AS THEY PLACED HIM in my arms I knew it had all been worth it," said Mira Sorvino, 42, who welcomed her third child, Holden, on June 22. The newcomer had had a difficult journey: Placenta previa required Sorvino to be hospitalized for weeks, and bed rest caused her to develop a blood clot. In all she spent nine "almost unbearable" weeks away from her children Mattea, 5, and Johnny, 3, and husband Christopher Backus. Then came serious delivery complications which led to a substantial loss of blood. "He is my miracle baby," said Sorvino. "With everything that threatened this pregnancy and both of our lives, he came out of it completely unscathed: perfectly healthy, beautiful and wonderful!"

TIGER WOODS *and* ELIN
———— ✴ ————
Charlie, February 8, 2009

He's won 14 major tournaments and is the best known athlete in the world. So what matters to Tiger Woods? "Being a father is the most significant thing I've ever done," says Woods, 34. "People say I was born to play golf, but I think I was born to be a dad."

He's getting even more practice since Charlie arrived to join Tiger, wife Elin, 30, and daughter Sam Alexis, 2, on Feb. 8. When it comes to parenting, Woods looks to what he learned from his father, Earl, who passed away in 2006. "How important it is to be there for the child, no matter what," he says. "To love them unconditionally. To earn their respect, earn their trust. All those things he did for me. Hopefully I'll be able to do that with my kids."

MEET THE CUBS
Tiger and Elin with Sam,
newcomer Charlie and
pooches Yogi (left) and Taz.

Garner, Affleck, Violet, 3, and Seraphina take a stroll in New York City on Oct. 4, 2009.

JENNIFER GARNER *and* BEN AFFLECK
*
Seraphina Rose Elizabeth, January 6, 2009

* MOLLY RINGWALD *and* PANIO GIANOPOULOS
Adele Georgiana and Roman Stylianos, July 10, 2009

TWINS? "YOU GET UP with one of the babies, feed and change that one and get the baby back to sleep, and the other wakes up and then you feed and change that one," Molly Ringwald, 41, said of her nocturnal routine, which sometimes includes singing her favorite jazz standards—"I'll Take Romance" and "Exactly Like You"—to newborns Adele and Roman. "It is exhausting, but it's wonderful."

Also much wished-for. Already a mom to now-6-year-old Mathilda with husband Panio Gianopoulos, 34, Ringwald, the '80s It Girl who starred in films such as *Sixteen Candles* and *Pretty in Pink,* didn't have an easy time getting pregnant. And then? "Having a son as well as another daughter," she said, "it was just a really grand surprise."

D on't be fooled by the big smile Jennifer Garner always sports whenever she's with her family. The actress says she's not nearly as together as she looks. "I fake it like any working mom, and I run out the door," said Garner at a premiere. "If you looked in my bag, there's a sippy cup in there right now."

Garner, 37, and husband Ben Affleck, 37, became parents for the second time in January with the birth of Seraphina Rose Elizabeth Affleck. Big sister Violet is now 4. On workdays, said the actress, "[I] feel like half my brain is somewhere else all the time, but when the camera's rolling, I pull it together and focus for two minutes, and then I kind of turn back to a ditz again. I have a split personality."

"WHEN WE FIRST STARTED TALKING ABOUT WANTING CHILDREN, HE WANTED TO WAIT UNTIL HE WAS 40. I SAID, 'OH, NO, THAT'S NOT GONNA WORK'"

"The babies are quiet," says Ringwald, whenever their big sister Mathilda (then 5) holds them.

When they welcomed daughter Harlow in January 2008, Nicole Richie and her boyfriend, Good Charlotte frontman Joel Madden, became cautious new parents. "Harlow was born into a home with two adults. We were so quiet with her; we made everything silent," recalled Richie. Times have changed. Their new son, Sparrow James Midnight Madden, "was born into a family," said Richie. "He's gotta hop on the train!"

The family home in L.A.'s Laurel Canyon may be Harlow's world, but the more mellow Sparrow seems perfectly happy napping in it. "He'll sleep through anything," said Madden. As for the unusual name, "it reminded me of the Johnny Cash song 'A Boy Named Sue,'" said Madden, 30. "My worry raising a son in Hollywood is what will he have to struggle for? I wanted to give him a name that he's going to have to stand up for. I love it. I think it's a beautiful name." Learning to care for two, says Richie, 28, is "a juggling act, but it's fun. I'm right where I belong."

"I'M GLAD I HAD A GIRL BEFORE I HAD A BOY. SHE JUST LOVES HIM SO MUCH"

So, Jennifer Hudson, how's mother-hood? "He's the cutest thing in the world!" raved the Grammy-winning singer, who gave birth to David Daniel Otunga Jr. on Aug. 10. "There are no words for it. He's the best. It's just amazing—us discovering each other, me becoming a mom."

And of course, he's brillia nt. "He's a very rare newborn," says Hudson. "He tries a lot—he's turning over, he's lifting up his own head,

he tries to hold his own bottle, sometimes I swear he's talking to me, or at least trying to. The other day he said 'Hi!'—I swear, I'm not crazy. David [fiancé David Otunga, 29] was there too, and he was like, 'He just said Hi!'" Little David, his mother says, is musical as well: "He seems like he's very interested. The other night he was having a screaming fit, and someone turns on the music and he just stops and calms down. Sometimes when he cries, I try to harmonize."

"Nobody," says O'Connell, "thinks I'm funnier than my daughters [do]."

"MOTHERHOOD HAS MADE ME MORE AFFECTIONATE, EMOTIONAL"

✳ REBECCA ROMIJN *and* JERRY O'CONNELL

**Dolly and Charlie,
December 28, 2008**

SHE LIKES THEM, SHE REALLY likes them: "Being a mom makes me feel whole and like I understand the meaning of life," said Rebecca Romijn, 37, sounding very much like almost every other new mother. "All I want to do is stare into my babies' eyes nonstop." Amazingly, Romijn took only four months to lose 60 lbs. she had gained before the December 2008 birth of twin girls Dolly Rebecca Rose and Charlie Tamara Tulip. And how was husband Jerry O'Connell, 35, responding to living in an otherwise all-estrogen household? "He's having such a blast with these girls," said Romijn—although, she added, "he's determined not to let them ever date while he is alive."

SARAH MICHELLE GELLAR *and* FREDDIE PRINZE Jr.

Charlotte Grace, September 19, 2009

It was a special—and especially mellow—delivery. "I went into labor at the gym!" recalled Sarah Michelle Gellar. "I didn't really believe it. I just felt a little nauseous, and my trainer said to me, 'Um, isn't your baby coming next week? Maybe it's time now?' I said, 'Oh, no, I doubt it . . .' I said to Freddie, 'This can't be labor.' He kept saying, 'Sarah, are you sure?'"

It was; Charlotte Grace arrived soon after. "Here's the other thing about the delivery: The epidural is fantastic," said Gellar. "No one tells you that with the epidural, there's just no pain. It was a very peaceful delivery." Other highlights? "She smiles all day long, and she is loving and cuddly. And now people are really going to hate me," jokes Gellar. "She doesn't cry. She will just go, 'Wah.' Once."

Gellar, 32, and Prinze, 33, married seven years, are thrilled to be parents but glad they waited a few years. "I'm so happy we didn't have kids in our 20s—I just didn't know a thing," said Prinze. "You have so much more patience in your 30s, and I feel like I appreciate this so much more. In your 20s you're still waking up and going, 'Oh my God, I can't believe I did that last night.' You've got to wait until you stop having those nights. It's so easy to be selfish in your 20s and not want to sacrifice. But now, I know I would do anything for Charlotte."

"I'm such a cliché right now," said Gellar, "but she is the greatest gift that anyone has ever given me."

KATHERINE HEIGL
and
JOSH KELLEY

———— ✹ ————

Nancy Leigh ("Naleigh"), November 23, 2008

On Sept. 16, her first day in Atlanta filming the romantic comedy *Life as We Know It*, a flustered Katherine Heigl appeared on the set with a mouthful of apologies—and a really good excuse. She had just adopted a Korean-born baby girl on very short notice (although she and her husband, country singer Josh Kelley, 29, had applied and been approved, they had expected a much longer wait. A sudden congratulations-you're-parents notification caught them by surprise).

"She was in an absolute panic initially," said her *Grey's Anatomy* costar Chandra Wilson. But when the couple met 10-month-old Naleigh on Sept. 10, "everything calmed down. You couldn't see someone more in love with her baby."

Heigl, whose sister Margaret Leigh, 34, was adopted from Korea, had always longed to adopt a child—and made it clear to Kelley when they met in 2005. "[Adoption is] really important to me," Heigl, 31, told Ellen DeGeneres. "I wanted to make sure I was marrying a guy . . . who understood that that was going to have to happen."

It did, and they're thrilled. "They are so funny and easygoing, and they'll share those qualities with this child," said one friend. "They are going to love big."

✳ MICHELLE *and* JIM BOB DUGGAR
Jordyn-Grace, December 18, 2008, 7 lbs. 3 oz.

MICHELLE AND JIM BOB DUGGAR of Tontitown, Ark., welcomed daughter Jordyn-Grace Makiya on Dec. 18, 2008, necessitating a title change in their TLC reality series from *17 Kids and Counting* to *18 Kids and Counting*. (Jordyn-Grace's sibling costars are: Joshua, 21; twins John-David and Jana, 19; Jill, 18; Jessa, 17; Jinger, 16; Joseph, 14; Josiah, 13; Joy-Anna, 12; twins Jedidiah and Jeremiah, 11; Jason, 9; James, 8; Justin, 7; Jackson, 5; Johannah, 4; and Jennifer, 2.) "We get a lot of people saying we're overpopulating the world," said Jim Bob, 44, a conservative Christian. "We don't worry about what other people think. We consider each child a blessing from God." Michelle, 43, is hoping for more. "I am savoring every little moment right now because Jordyn-Grace could be my last baby," she said, her eyes welling up a bit. "I'd love to have more, but we'll have to see if it's possible."

(It was: As this book was going to press, Michelle was pregnant and due in March 2010.)

How they've changed

Transformations 2009: Celebs got slimmer, bigger, confronted cancer and—in one case—switched genders

The night before Valerie Bertinelli prepared to step out in public wearing a bikini—for the first time in nearly 30 years—she slept fitfully. Finally, she told herself, "What am I so afraid of? Come on—it's just a bathing suit!"

Well, yes and no. It *is* just a couple of strips of Lycra, but they're a couple of strips of Lycra that can irrationally rattle almost any woman. Additionally, Bertinelli was about to turn 49; had, only two years earlier, weighed 172 lbs.; and she was scheduled to reveal herself in said bikini live on *The Oprah Winfrey Show*. Insomnia seemed like a reasonable response.

Bertinelli's route to beach-body bravado started in 2007, when—as a spokeswoman for Jenny Craig—she began to shed 40 lbs. in nine months. Inspired, she decided to push further, continuing her diet and working out on her own—mostly walking 10,000 steps a day. Four months before her b-day, she hired a personal trainer and began running and strength training—and eventually dropped to 123 lbs. "I'm happy," she said. "I feel really good for my age." And? "I never, ever, ever had deltoids!" she says. "Oh my God, when I'm doing exercises and I see them pop out, I'm like, 'Yes!'"

Bertinelli says she hopes to keep to about 125 lbs., and that there's a "stake in the ground" at 132. A lot of the challenge, she says, is mental. "I'm just one jalapeño popper away from being 40 lbs. heavier again—that's what still resonates in my head."

THEN Bertinelli (left, in 2007) dropped 49 lbs. and toned her muscles.

"WHEN . . . I SEE [MY DELTOIDS] POP OUT, I'M LIKE, 'YES!'"

VALERIE BERTINELLI

CHRISTINA
APPLEGATE
✹

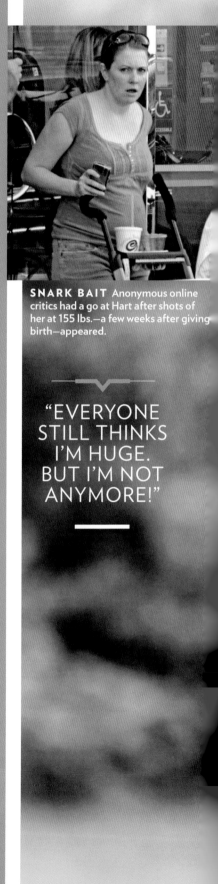

SNARK BAIT Anonymous online critics had a go at Hart after shots of her at 155 lbs.—a few weeks after giving birth—appeared.

"EVERYONE STILL THINKS I'M HUGE. BUT I'M NOT ANYMORE!"

Courage and Class

An actress copes with breast cancer and surgery

Talk about grace under pressure. Within weeks of undergoing a double mastectomy to battle breast cancer, Christina Applegate, 38, was onstage at the Emmys. "You have to get through the physical transformations, then buck up, go to work and try to be the normal, happy Christina," Applegate, who has remained cancer-free for more than a year, told PEOPLE in May, when she graced the cover of the 100 Most Beautiful issue.

Following her diagnosis, she experienced "a roller coaster of emotions. But there was a calm about what I had to do," she said. Reconstructive surgery, she says, was "hard. You don't look the same anymore.... None of the women I know [who have undergone similar surgery] are like, 'Yay, I love my boobs!' But you have to embrace them. It's a decision that you made to save your life." On the plus side, "I don't have to wear a bra!" she jokes. "And the gals look good in tank tops, and they didn't before."

✳ MELISSA JOAN HART

WHEN UNFLATTERING bathing-suit shots—taken only three months after she gave birth to her second son—showed up online and led to cruel Internet attacks about her body (one blog even blasted her for "giving pregnancy a bad name"), Melissa Joan Hart was devastated. "I still read blogs about me discussing how fat I've become," the 5'2" star said. "Everyone still thinks I'm huge. But I'm not anymore!" That's because after seeing those shots, the then-155-lb. star buckled down and shed a whopping 42 lbs. Now down to 110 lbs., she's "in the best shape of my life," she says.

How? Said Hart: "It was as hard for me as it would be for anyone else." Especially because she refused to commit to the 4:30 a.m. workouts that had kept her trim during her teen years on the hit shows *Clarissa Explains It All* and *Sabrina, the Teenage Witch.* "I didn't want to take any time away from spending it with my sons," she said.

Hart, 33, says she was "lucky" to be able to consult a nutritionist and a trainer, but said that her biggest inspiration came from the women around her—including friend Jaime Pressly, who has a son, Dezi, 2, as well as her own mom, Paula, 53, who gave birth to seven children "and is tiny!" Hart said. "I realized I don't have to be heavy just because I have kids.

"I never thought I'd pose in a bikini again," Hart added, noting that her last scantily clad photo shoot was a decade ago. "To do it two kids and 10 years later? I'm so proud!"

KIRSTIE
ALLEY

"WHEN I LOOK
AT MYSELF,
I GO, 'UGH,
I'M THIS HUGE
LOSER!'"

Once More unto the Gym

Having regained her lost weight—and more—Kirstie Alley vows to try again

When Kirstie Alley stepped on the scale early this year, for the first time in 15 months, she had a hunch that it wouldn't be pretty. "I got on the scale and started screaming," Alley recalled. "It said 228 lbs., which is my highest weight ever. I was so much more disgusting than I thought!"

The discovery was especially unnerving because Alley, 58, had managed to famously lose 75 lbs. and maintain a weight of 145 lbs. during her three-year stint as a Jenny Craig spokeswoman. Alas, she and Jenny Craig parted ways in December 2007, and since then the *Fat Actress* actress had not worked out. As for her diet, Jenny Craig's small, low-calorie portions gave way to Chinese takeout and pasta drenched in butter, butter, butter. "I fell off the horse. I actually fell off the Trojan horse!" says the 5'8" star. "But your solution is either jump under the E train or you do it all again."

As for her plan this time around, she says, "I am creating a weight-loss system that will end the rollercoaster ride. Details are completely under wraps."

ENCORE
Fretting she had "let all these people down," Alley said she would do better.

CHANGING
Chastity Bono then (inset, in '93) and Chaz Bono in November.

✳ CHAZ BONO

SHE WAS THE ADORABLE moppet who said "Good night everybody and God bless" at the end of her parents' TV variety show. Later on, at 26, Chastity Bono, the daughter of Sonny and Cher, came out as gay. This year her life took another dramatic turn: Around her 40th birthday, Chastity Bono began undergoing a sex change and became Chaz. "After many years of consideration, he has made the courageous decision to honor his true identity," said Bono's spokesman Howard Bragman. "He is proud of his decision and grateful for the support and respect that has already been shown by his loved ones."

Cher sounded like any loving mother trying to absorb big but unusual news. "Chaz is embarking on a difficult journey, but one that I will support," she said. "I respect the courage it takes to go through this transition in the glare of public scrutiny, and although I may not understand, I will strive to be understanding. The one thing that will never change is my abiding love for my child."

For Chaz, 40, living openly as a man is part of the transition process, as is taking testosterone. He also plans to have surgery, which may include a double mastectomy.

Chaz's longtime girlfriend, grad student Jennifer Elia, 34, is sticking by him through the transition. "Jen is very tolerant and respectful," says Chaz's friend Bruce Vilanch. "I think that they both really felt that they'd found the person they were meant to be with."

JESSICA SIMPSON
and TONY ROMO

Bye-bye love

*Jessica Simpson and Tony Romo hit
the rocks in '09—and they weren't alone*

Barbie and Ken, it seems, will not be building their Malibu dream house.

The night before Jessica Simpson and Dallas Cowboys quarterback Tony Romo were to celebrate her 29th birthday with a Barbie-and-Ken-themed bash at her parents' Encino, Calif., home, Romo dumped Simpson, his girlfriend of almost two years. Neither said what had precipitated the split, but marital pressure may have played a role. "She expected [an engagement] ring for her birthday," said a Simpson source. "Sometimes in those situations, it's 'Put up or shut up,' and he decided he wasn't ready."

Additionally, some Dallas fans—postulating that Simpson was a potent distraction—had questioned Romo's dedication to football, and Romo, 29, may have felt he had to make a choice. "This is crunch time," said a Romo pal, noting that Cowboys training was only two weeks away. "I definitely think he's fully committed and focused on being the best quarterback he can be." Simpson's *closerthanthis* relationship with her parents may also have played a role. "It's hard for anyone who is with Jess," said a friend of Simpson's. "She doesn't have boundaries with her parents. She tells them everything. So you have two extra people in your relationship knowing everything that is going on. When you have a fight, it's not just between the two of you. Everyone is weighing in."

Hoping to move on, Simpson focused on her VH1 show *The Price of Beauty*. Halfway through the NFL season, Dallas—with Romo at quarterback—had a winning record.

✳ LEANN RIMES
and DEAN SHEREMET

LEANN RIMES AND HER husband, dancer Dean Sheremet, 29, double dated with actor Eddie Cibrian and his wife, Brandi Glanville, 37, while Rimes and Glanville were shooting a Lifetime network movie, *Northern Lights*, together—and Glanville thought she detected the singer flirting with her husband. "Girls get that way with my husband all the time—he's a good-looking guy," she said. "=But it was different this time. It was a little more reciprocated."

Chalk one up for intuition. Within months, Rimes had left Sheremet, and, said Glanville, she and Cibrian were headed for divorce as well. (When Rimes called her one day, said Glanville, she told the singer, "He's all yours.")

Long rumored to be a couple, Rimes, 27, and Cibrian, 36, went public with their romance in August, when they were photographed playing golf and attending a Kings of Leon concert.

MEL *and* ROBYN
GIBSON

"THE REAL
MEDAL GOES
TO MY WIFE,
WHO'S A
WONDERFUL
WOMAN"

Mrs. Mad Max says "Enough"

*After 28 years of triumph and drama,
Robyn Gibson quietly files for divorce*

They were one of Hollywood's most private, and long-lasting, couples, sticking together through 28 years, seven children and his wild behavior. "The real medal goes to my wife, who's a wonderful woman," Mel Gibson told Diane Sawyer in 2004.

But all was not as it seemed. Gibson, 53, his wife Robyn, 53, and many of his children and several grandchildren regularly attended Mass together at Holy Family Chapel, the church he built near their Malibu home. But on Easter, a forlorn Mel showed up alone. Afterward, he told parishioners, "Well, she filed for divorce."

Later, Gibson revealed that he and Robyn had, in fact, been quietly separated since August 2006, less than a month after he was pulled over for drunken driving in Malibu and made anti-Semitic remarks to his arresting officer (he later apologized and entered rehab). In her April 13 divorce filing, Robyn cited "irreconcilable differences" and requested joint custody of Tom, 10, the only child still under 18 of their six sons and one daughter.

A possible catalyst for Robyn's decision became clear on May 25, when Gibson acknowledged that he was about to become a father again, with Russian-born singer Oksana Grigorieva, 39. Their baby girl, Lucia, was born on Oct. 30 in L.A.

MEL NOW
Gibson and girlfriend Oksana Grigorieva welcomed a daughter, Lucia, in October.

CHRIS EVERT *and* GREG NORMAN
✳

Game, Set, Mismatc

A once-trumpeted love ends on a big, honking flat note

It began with drama, arced through a romantic fantasy and ended with a resounding *splat*.

Golfer Greg Norman and former tennis star Andy Mill were good buddies—until, in 2006, Norman and Chris Evert, Mill's wife of 18 years, fell in love. When the dust settled, Mill and Evert had divorced, Norman had split from *his* wife of 25 years, Laura Andrassy, 60, and Norman and Evert, both 54, had married in an elegant June 2008 ceremony in the Bahamas.

Fifteen months later, it was over. Why? "Greg got in between Andy and his sons, which caused a great deal of turmoil for Chris," said a close source. "On one occasion, Andy flew from his Aspen home to Boca Raton to spend time with his sons, and before Andy even touched ground, Greg whisked Nicky off in his private jet. He took him to his own ranch in Colorado, leaving a very unhappy Andy crying on the phone to his son." Added a South Florida friend of the couple: "Chris had a midlife crisis and came out of it totally turned on by Greg's celebrity, gorgeous looks and bank account. They didn't take time to get to know each other. Both of them are narcissistic and want to control. In a celebrity marriage, only one person can be like that."

One winner in all this? Andy Mill, 55, who recently became engaged to Aspen homemaker Debra Harvick, 40. "Now that Greg is out of the picture, we are all fine, and I am ecstatic," said Mill. "Chrissy and I are friends."

✳ LINDSAY LOHAN *and* SAMANTHA RONSON

OFF AGAIN, ON AGAIN. Then on again, and off again. Then some uncertainty—perhaps even among the people involved—whether it was on again. Or, just maybe, off. Again. For the first half of 2009, keeping up with the current romantic status of Lindsay Lohan, 23, and deejay Samantha Ronson, 32, was a little like fast-forwarding through a Ping-Pong match: A person could get whiplash just watching.

By mid-June, though, the romance seemed to be in a seriously dormant stage, with a friend of Ronson's saying it was, like, totally over. "Sam let Lindsay back into her life as a friend, but now even a friendship seems impossible," said the source. "No matter how many times she promises to change, Lindsay loses control and starts acting like a maniac."

As for June photos of the two together, "Sam is a nice person and wouldn't throw anyone out of her life, but it was no more than that."

> ## "LINDSAY LOSES CONTROL AND STARTS ACTING LIKE A MANIAC"
> **—A FRIEND**

PLAY IT AGAIN, SAM Sometimes, deejay Samantha Ronson and Lohan made beautiful music together.

✳ A V R I L L A V I G N E
and D E R Y C K W H I B L E Y

WHAT, NO MUD? Avril Lavigne's split from her husband of three years, Sum 41 lead singer Deryck Whibley, was far more polite than it was punk. Although each had been seen partying with other people in the months leading up to their divorce announcement, they sounded like a pair of Hallmark cards when discussing the impending dissolution.

"Deryck and I have been together for 6½ years," Lavigne, 25, wrote on her Web site. "We have been friends since I was 17, started dating when I was 19 and married when I was 21. I am grateful for our time together, and I am grateful and blessed for our remaining friendship." Whibley, 29, who continued to help produce Lavigne's next album even as the marriage was sputtering, wrote on his MySpace page, "Our decision to part ways is amicable, and she holds a special place in my heart and forever will be a great and amazing friend."

Bouncing Back

They hadn't set a date, but in May 2008 Jennifer Love Hewitt was testing her housewife potential with fiancé Ross McCall, 33, she said, by "fixing up the house and making him dinner. I'm not a 1952 kind of gal all the way round, but little spurts of it are fine!"

And then . . . they broke up over the Christmas holidays, surprising even their friends. Hewitt, however, bounced back quickly: In April 2009 she told Ellen DeGeneres that she was dating her *Ghost Whisperer* costar Jamie Kennedy, 39. "I've heard about it—about being friends with somebody and it turns into something else, and I've never really done that before and it's been great," said Hewitt, 30. "And [Kennedy] really saw who I was as a person more than anybody had ever done in my whole life."

USHER *and*
TAMEKA FOSTER
RAYMOND
✴

Ushered Out

*After a tumultuous courtship, a delayed wedding and a
volatile two years, the couple surprise no one by calling it a day*

U sher may be losing a wife, but he's gaining songwriting material. Rapidly.

To recap: The singer, now 31, and longtime love Tameka Foster, 38, then pregnant with his son, had planned to marry in July 2007, but on the morning of the nuptials the wedding was canceled. Friends blamed, among other things, Usher's cold feet; haggling over a prenup (Foster eventually signed); a recent revelation that Foster had once been arrested for car theft; and venom between Foster and Usher's mother, and former manager, Jonnetta Patton.

One week later Usher and Tameka wed; Usher's mother was not there.

In the ensuing months the couple defended their love. Said Tameka: "I can finally share my dreams. And because of that, I know that man loves me." Said Usher: "[Getting married] and having a child is something that everyone should celebrate. What's happened to us as a culture and a people?"

August 2008: Usher rehires his mother as his manager.

February 2009: Tameka suffers a heart attack while being anesthetized prior to liposuction in São Paulo.

June 2009: Usher files for divorce.

October 2009: Usher releases a new song, "Papers," with the lyric, "For you I gave my heart and turned my back against the world/... I done damn near lost my mama, I done been through so much drama/ ... I'm ready to sign them papers."

Rebound Romances?

Is it love? Limbo? Hasta la vista? Only time will tell

✳ PRINCE HARRY
and CHELSY DAVY

BREAK UP THEN MAKE UP seems to be the rhythm of romance for younger Windsors. In 2007 Prince William and Kate Middleton fractured, only to mend two months later. Now Prince Harry and Chelsy Davy are roller-coastering: They split in January, then quickly began retesting the waters (including, according to a London paper, an African photo safari planned for New Year's). If Davy, 24, and Harry reignite, he can afford a nice reunion gift: When he turned 25 Sept. 15, Harry gained access to some of the $10.5 million left to him by his mother, Princess Diana.

✳ NICK LACHEY
and VANESSA
MINNILLO

IN JUNE REPS FOR Lachey, 36, and Minnillo, 29, confirmed the romance was a wrap.

And then . . . at the end of August, they decided that staring into each other's eyes in an L.A. bar was the right thing to do. Next, going to a party together in Manhattan seemed like the right thing to do. After that, they were at a Cincinnati club, the Righteous Room, doing the right thing yet again.

What does it all mean? "Nick and Vanessa are not officially back together, but they're hanging out," a source says. "They'll see what happens. . . . They're not exclusive right now."

Slumdog

Surprise

2009 at the movies: vampires, a Mumbai musical and more

THE MULTIPLEX HOSTED GIANT ROBOTS, bloodsuckers and the return of Mr. Spock. So who would have guessed that the biggest surprise of 2009, and biggest Oscar-winner since *Lord of the Rings: Return of the King* in 2003, would be a heartwarming, suspension-of-disbelief-enabling confection that answers, resoundingly in the affirmative, the age-old question: Can a kid from the Mumbai slums survive gangsters, win *Who Wants to Be a Millionaire?*, find love and lead a song-and-dance number at the Mumbai train station?

Up

BY TAKING RISKS—one four-minute segment contains no dialogue but can move viewers to tears—Pixar broke new ground in digital animation (and profit: *Up* grossed $292,979,556). And who doesn't love a talkative mutt with maybe a bit of ADD ("Squirrel!")?

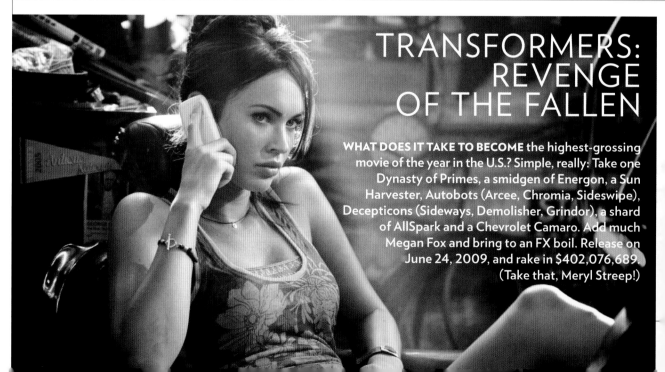

TRANSFORMERS: REVENGE OF THE FALLEN

WHAT DOES IT TAKE TO BECOME the highest-grossing movie of the year in the U.S.? Simple, really: Take one Dynasty of Primes, a smidgen of Energon, a Sun Harvester, Autobots (Arcee, Chromia, Sideswipe), Decepticons (Sideways, Demolisher, Grindor), a shard of AllSpark and a Chevrolet Camaro. Add much Megan Fox and bring to an FX boil. Release on June 24, 2009, and rake in $402,076,689. (Take that, Meryl Streep!)

THE HANGOVER

WE CAN HEAR THE PITCH NOW: "Three guys wake up glazed in Vegas after an epic bachelor party, look around and notice there's a tiger in the bathroom, a baby in a closet and a groom nowhere to be found." Like a game of Clue played in reverse, the trio sort it out with help from a stripper, Mike Tyson and Taser-wielding cops. Bradley Cooper starred; Zach Galifianakis stole scenes. Gross: $277,069,721.

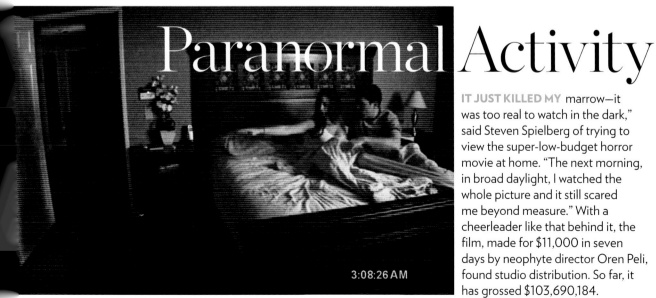

Paranormal Activity

IT JUST KILLED MY marrow—it was too real to watch in the dark," said Steven Spielberg of trying to view the super-low-budget horror movie at home. "The next morning, in broad daylight, I watched the whole picture and it still scared me beyond measure." With a cheerleader like that behind it, the film, made for $11,000 in seven days by neophyte director Oren Peli, found studio distribution. So far, it has grossed $103,690,184.

3:08:26 AM

Julie & Julia

THE FIRST FILM BASED on a blog, *J&J* gloried in romance, butter and Meryl at her Streepiest—alive, funny and delightfully over-the-top, portraying *Mastering the Art of French Cooking* author Julia Child. "[To say] she has outdone herself is only to say that she's done it again," wrote one critic. Audiences ate it up, to the tune of $93,723,567.

PAUL BLART: MALL COP

MOVIES: THEY CAN BE artistic, inspiring, inventive. Or, they can be *Paul Blart: Mall Cop* (with Kevin James, left), and simply make lots and lots of money. Callously ignoring critics ("*Blart* is just empty calories," said one), millions plopped down, reached for the popcorn and helped this family-friendly comedy—made for a modest $26 million—gross $146,336,178.

MOON STRUCK Volturi guard Felix (Daniel Cudmore) lords it over Edward Cullen (Robert Pattinson)— temporarily.

The Twilight Saga:
New Moon

GIRLS WENT FOR *Hannah Montana: The Movie*; their big sisters—and moms and hipper aunts—swarmed *New Moon*, the second in the film series based on Stephenie Meyer's best-selling vampires-as-metaphor *Twilight* books. The opening weekend—$140,700,000—was the third best in Hollywood history, as hordes of Twi-hard fans watched the undead and the merely uncertain struggle, mightily and moodily, to resist temptation.

HANNAH MONTANA: THE MOVIE

LITTLE GIRLS—AND THEIR tween sisters—rule huge swaths of the entertainment world, and Miley Cyrus still captivated their hearts (and the contents of their Hannah Montana purses). A full three years after the premiere of her Disney show—an epoch in the teen-idol world—Cyrus, 17, saw her movie make more money ($79,566,871) than any other G-rated film of 2009.

AN EDUCATION

AS A WHIP-SMART reincarnation of Audrey Hepburn, Carey Mulligan portrays Jenny, a French-obsessed '60s British schoolgirl destined for Oxford intellectualism when an older man, Peter Sarsgaard, distracts her with a weekend jaunt to her beloved Paris, immersing Jenny into his fabulous but shady world. Her performance is *magnifique*.

Star Trek

AS EVERYONE IN Hollywood knows: The eleventh time is a charm. Okay, not really, but that only makes director J.J. Abrams' achievement more remarkable. Boldly going where lots of men had gone before, he revivified a franchise many assumed dead—and in the process made the eleventh *Star Trek* movie (with Chris Pine, left, and Zachary Quinto) the series' highest-grossing ever ($257,704,099).

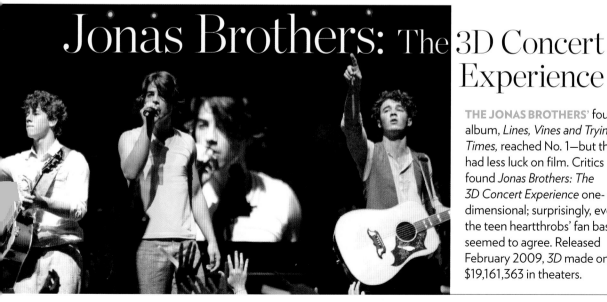

Jonas Brothers: The 3D Concert Experience

THE JONAS BROTHERS' fourth album, *Lines, Vines and Trying Times,* reached No. 1—but they had less luck on film. Critics found *Jonas Brothers: The 3D Concert Experience* one-dimensional; surprisingly, even the teen heartthrobs' fan base seemed to agree. Released February 2009, *3D* made only $19,161,363 in theaters.

REUNITED
"People are entitled to their own opinions, but people burned me a little more than I was expecting," said Jason (with Molly in Queenstown, New Zealand). "What I had to do was right for everyone involved."

The Bachelor

NOT ACTUALLY LOVE
Former *Bachelorette* suitor Jason Mesnick, a single man with washboard abs, earnest eyes and a cute little son, seemed the rightest of Mr. Rights to fans of the ABC series. That fantasy ended when he went on national TV and—classic reality moment!—dumped the woman he'd chosen, Melissa Rycroft (top right). Instead he confessed he really cared for Molly Malaney (bottom), pick No. 2. Melissa called him a "bastard," but she recovered: She was a hit on *Dancing with the Stars* and accepted a marriage proposal from a former sweetheart. Jason and Molly became engaged too. *Que sera, sera.*

Television

Talk show hosts were all the buzz, Paula Abdul turned into Ellen DeGeneres, and an Office romance led—at last—to the altar

CONAN SHIFTS

FALLON ARRIVES

Night Moves

The air was thick all year with media gossip about NBC's league of talk show gentlemen. Jay Leno, the No. 1 star in late-night programming, retired as host of NBC's *Tonight Show* on May 29 after 17 years. Conan O'Brien, who'd lasted almost as long as the host of *Late Night* despite early predictions that he was doomed, inherited Leno's job. His old show was taken over by former *Saturday Night Live* star Jimmy Fallon. Then Jay, whom no one expected to spend a quiet life raising cantaloupe, resurfaced: He launched a weeknight show much like his old one, only now it aired at 10 p.m. to anemic ratings. At which point Jay was asked if he'd ever go back to *Tonight.* "If that's what they wanted . . . sure."

GLEE

HAPPILY EVER AFTER The brightest TV hit of the year, FOX's new comedy drama is an ingenious distillation of pop-music phenomena like *High School Musical* and *American Idol*. A winkingly campy melodrama about a competitive teenage singing society, *Glee* is sprinkled with gleefully malicious humor aimed at adults—most of it supplied by actress Jane Lynch as monstrous cheerleading coach Sue Sylvester. But the big, bright bursts of music are what matter most: The cast's weekly covers of songs, from Carrie Underwood's "Last Name" to "Maybe This Time" from *Cabaret,* became iTunes hits. And *Glee* has cheered up anyone worried about the future of American musicals: A suspenseful high point involved two kids dueling with a song from *Wicked.*

Oprah Winfrey

OMG! The most powerful woman in all of television announced the end of an era—*her* era. With a long-term plan of establishing her own network based out of L.A., Oprah Winfrey said in November that she wouldn't extend her nationally syndicated Chicago talk show any further and set a final air date, Sept. 9, 2011. Ending the program almost precisely 25 years since its debut "feels right in my bones and it feels right in my spirit," said Winfrey, whose total worth was recently estimated at $2.3 billion. "It's the perfect number." Tom Cruise is just gonna have to find a new couch.

THE GLENN BECK SHOW

CRAZY LIKE A FOX An emotionally and politically volatile new star in the punditry galaxy, Beck entertained and/or appalled viewers with just about the most outlandish display ever put on by a commentator: He cried, chortled with glee and talked in funny voices while, among other things, accusing President Obama of railroading the country into socialism. Jon Stewart attacked him, and Sarah Palin thanked him in her book. Beck titled his own bestseller *Arguing with Idiots.*

The Office

I, DUNDER, TAKE THEE, MIFFLIN There have always been two real human beings with real beating hearts on NBC's *The Office*: Jim (John Krasinski) and his pregnant girlfriend Pam (Jenna Fischer). Jim and Pam finally tied the knot in an hour-long episode that included a great sight gag: The couple's office mates decided to copy the entrance procession of th "JK" wedding video that had been an online viral sensation. A dorky yet touching moment As Fischer told PEOPLE: "All the romance, all of the love and tons and tons of crazy."

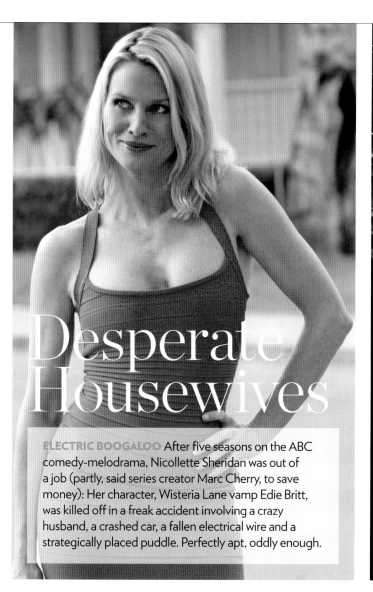

Desperate Housewives

ELECTRIC BOOGALOO After five seasons on the ABC comedy-melodrama, Nicollette Sheridan was out of a job (partly, said series creator Marc Cherry, to save money): Her character, Wisteria Lane vamp Edie Britt, was killed off in a freak accident involving a crazy husband, a crashed car, a fallen electrical wire and a strategically placed puddle. Perfectly apt, oddly enough.

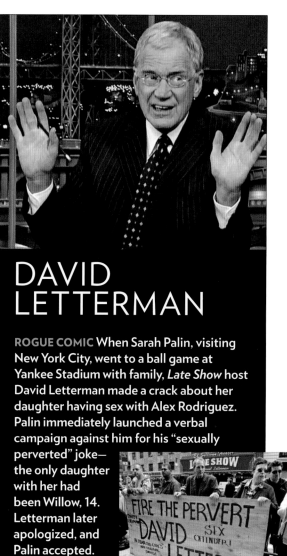

DAVID LETTERMAN

ROGUE COMIC When Sarah Palin, visiting New York City, went to a ball game at Yankee Stadium with family, *Late Show* host David Letterman made a crack about her daughter having sex with Alex Rodriguez. Palin immediately launched a verbal campaign against him for his "sexually perverted" joke— the only daughter with her had been Willow, 14. Letterman later apologized, and Palin accepted.

AMERICAN IDOL

JUDGMENT DAY The pop world was brought to a halt by a tweet Aug. 4: "With sadness in my heart, I've decided not to return. . . ." *American Idol* judge Paula Abdul was announcing her decision to leave the FOX juggernaut. A month later Ellen DeGeneres agreed to join the show. "Think of all the money I'll save from not having to text in my vote," she joked. Abdul wished her replacement good luck and, having fun with all the fuss (far right), impersonated DeGeneres on the *VH1 Divas* concert.

The Year in Music

Taylor Swift reigns, Lady Gaga mixes camp and vamp, and Britney officially joins the circus

NINETEEN-YEAR-OLD COUNTRY superstar Taylor Swift can look back on a bad moment and a great year. At the VMAs, as she accepted the Best Female Video award for "You Belong with Me," Kanye West grabbed her mic and announced that the prize should have gone elsewhere—disgracing himself in front of millions. (Tweeted singer John Rich: "He needs to have his @@@ kicked . . . right now!") West later apologized, saying he was "ashamed."

Taylor recovered, Swiftly: In November, at the Country Music Awards, she won four—and became the youngest person ever named Entertainer of the Year.

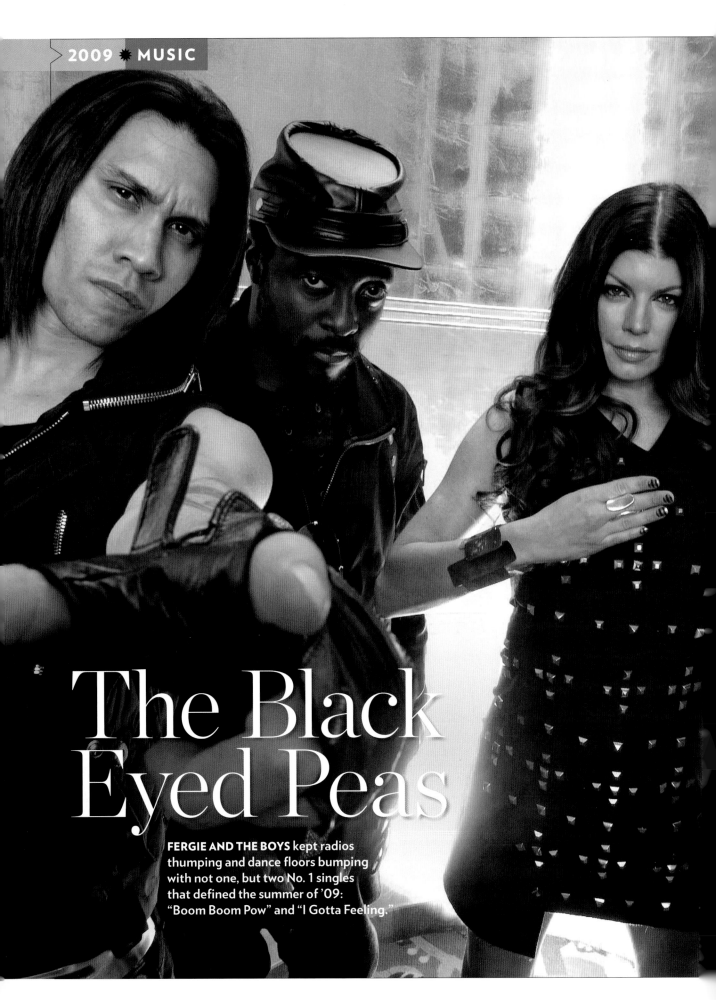

The Black Eyed Peas

FERGIE AND THE BOYS kept radios thumping and dance floors bumping with not one, but two No. 1 singles that defined the summer of '09: "Boom Boom Pow" and "I Gotta Feeling."

Kings of Leon

THE YEAR BEGAN for these Nashville rockers—three brothers and a cousin—with a Grammy win for "Sex on Fire." But they would really set the charts ablaze with "Use Somebody," a soaring ballad that seemed to touch the sky.

THE BEATLES

FOUR DECADES after their breakup, the Beatles had a great year. Abbey Road Studios released *The Beatles*, a beautiful remastering of 14 albums; for more active wannaBeatles, the game *The Beatles: Rock Band* hit stores.

Whitney Houston

BACK IN FULL DIVA EFFECT, Houston went a long way toward erasing the reality-show memory of *Being Bobby Brown* with her comeback album, *I Look to You*. Debuting atop the charts, the CD showed why fans fell in love with her voice in the first place.

MAXWELL

IT HAD BEEN eight long years since this neo-soul star's last disc. But he got his groove back and then some with the sexy sounds of his No. 1 album *BLACKsummers'-night* and its long-running hit "Pretty Wings."

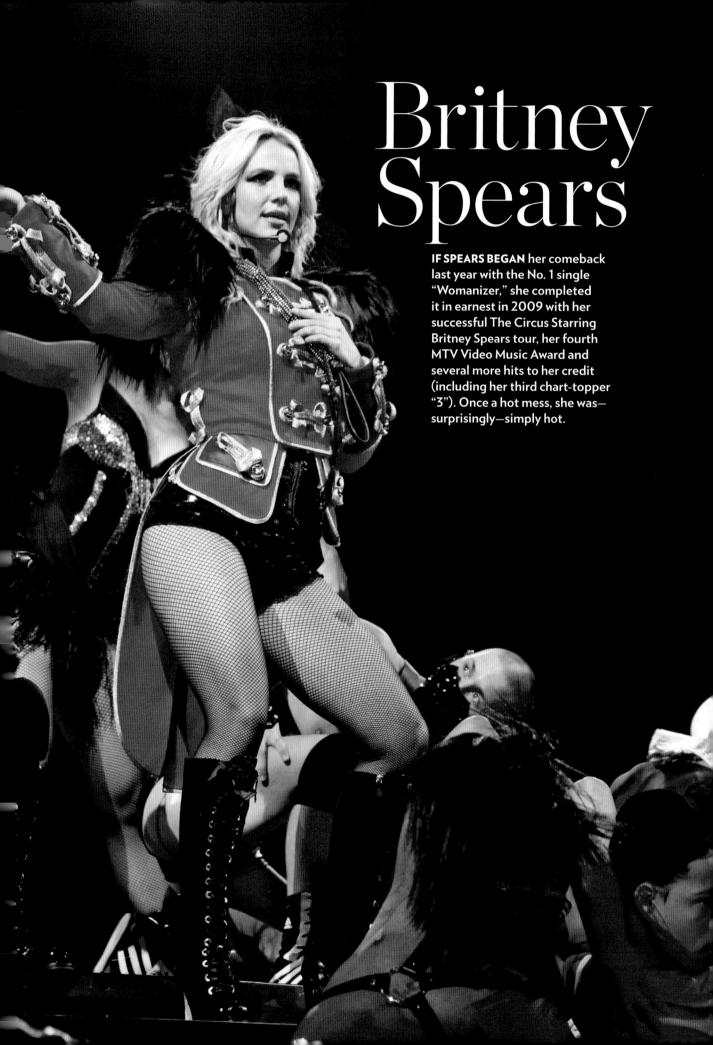

Britney Spears

IF SPEARS BEGAN her comeback last year with the No. 1 single "Womanizer," she completed it in earnest in 2009 with her successful The Circus Starring Britney Spears tour, her fourth MTV Video Music Award and several more hits to her credit (including her third chart-topper "3"). Once a hot mess, she was— surprisingly—simply hot.

Lady Gaga

SHE'S STEFANI Germanotta to her family, but Lady Gaga to millions who like their dance music with a side of outrageous. How did this happen? "I was the nerdball in theater and chorus," she says of her years at an all-girls school in N.Y.C. Only 23, she broke big out of the club scene and scored four No. 1 hits in 2009, including "Paparazzi." Not shy, she titled her inaugural jaunt as a headliner *The Fame Ball Tour*.

PENELOPE
CRUZ

OSCARS
Dress by Vintage Pierre Balmain

Best in show

Sexy, sleek and stunning, couture confections in dramatic silhouettes dominated the Hollywood party circuit. But not everyone can be a red carpet winner: Here are the year's fashion faves...and flops

✳ and worst

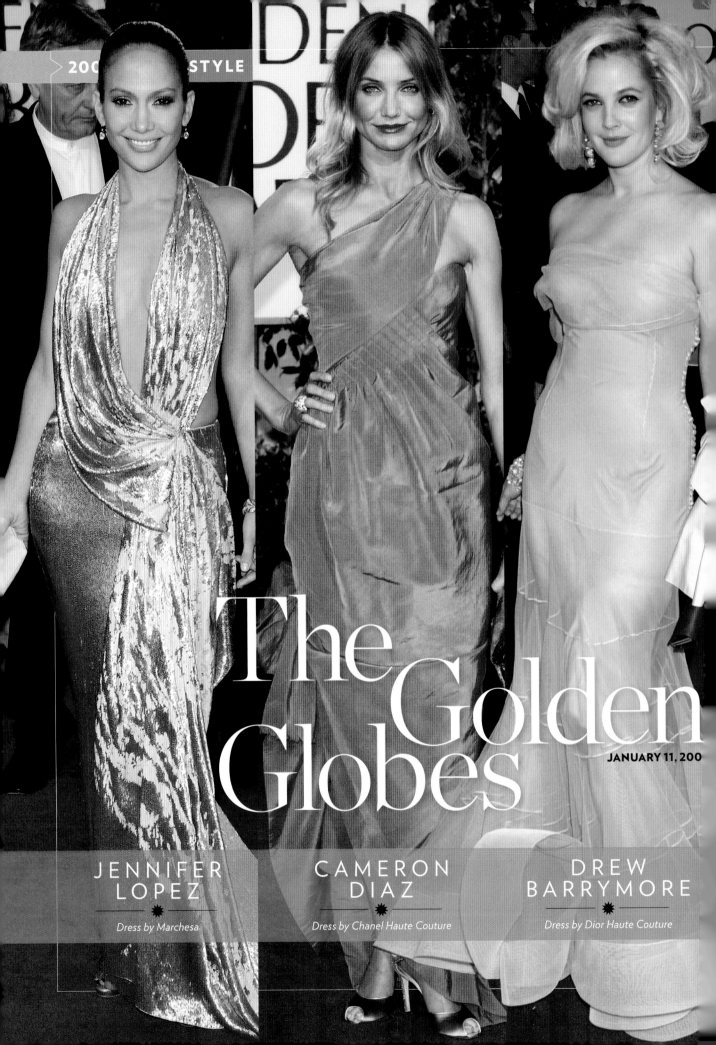

The Golden Globes

JANUARY 11, 200

JENNIFER LOPEZ

✺

Dress by Marchesa

CAMERON DIAZ

✺

Dress by Chanel Haute Couture

DREW BARRYMORE

✺

Dress by Dior Haute Couture

EVA
MENDES

*

Dress by Dior

ANGELINA
JOLIE

*

Dress by Atelier Versace

OLIVIA
WILDE

*

Dress by Reem Acra

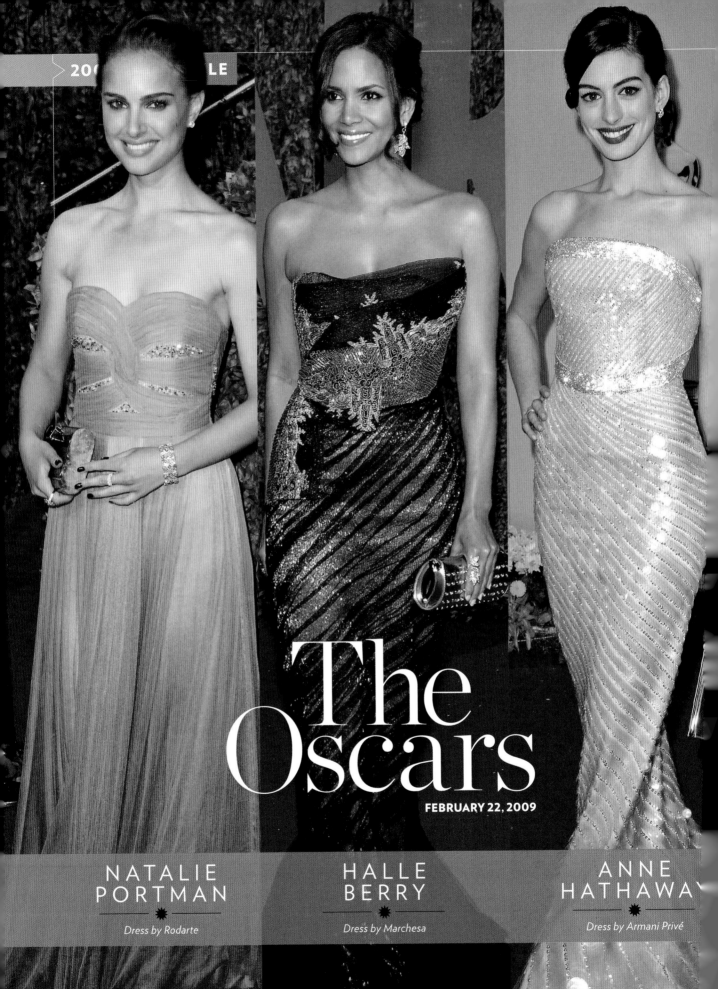

The Oscars

FEBRUARY 22, 2009

NATALIE
PORTMAN

Dress by Rodarte

HALLE
BERRY

Dress by Marchesa

ANNE
HATHAWAY

Dress by Armani Privé

REESE
THERSPOON

Dress by Rodarte

SARAH JESSICA
PARKER

Dress by Dior Couture

ANGELINA
JOLIE

Dress by Elie Saab Couture

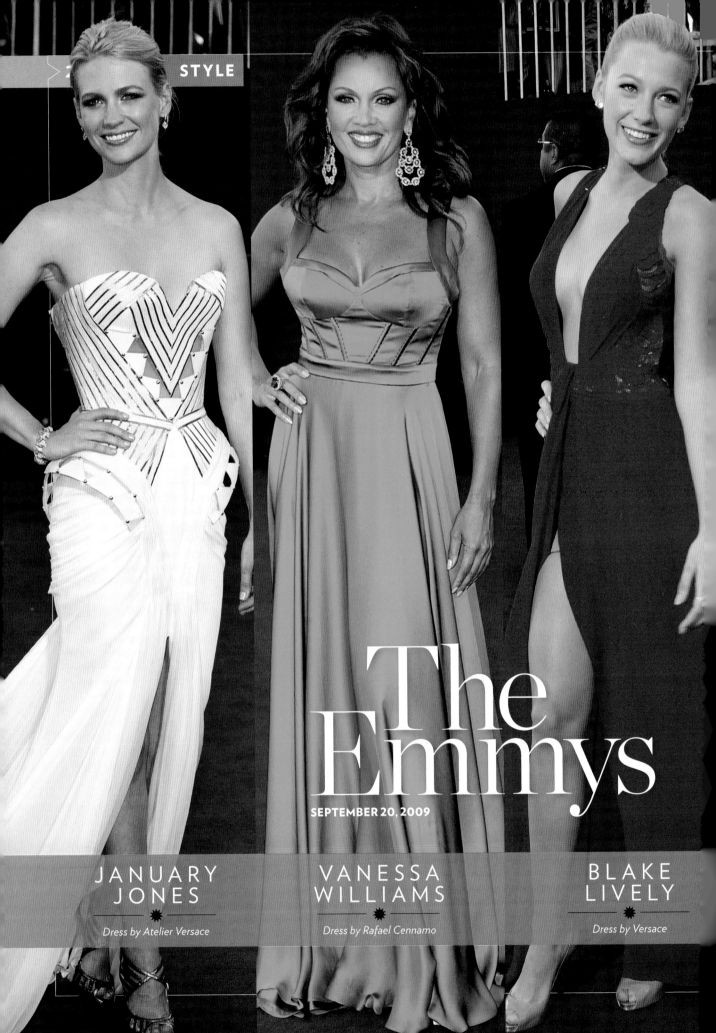

The Emmys

SEPTEMBER 20, 2009

JANUARY
JONES

Dress by Atelier Versace

VANESSA
WILLIAMS

Dress by Rafael Cennamo

BLAKE
LIVELY

Dress by Versace

HEIDI
KLUM
✳
Dress by Marchesa

DREW
BARRYMORE
✳
Dress by Monique Lhuillier

LEIGHTON
MEESTER
✳
Dress by Bottega Veneta

The Grammys

FEBRUARY 8, 2009

CARRIE
UNDERWOOD

*

Dress by Zuhair Murad

MILEY
CYRUS

*

Dress by Hervé Léger by Max Azria

AUDRINA
PATRIDGE

*

Dress by Tadashi

TAYLOR
SWIFT

Dress by Kaufman Franco

LEONA
LEWIS

Dress by Randi Rahm Couture

KATY
PERRY

Dress by Basil Soda

SAG

JANUARY 25, 2009

CHRISTINA
APPLEGATE

✳

Dress by Emanuel Ungaro

PENELOPE
CRUZ

✳

Dress by Azzedine Alaïa

KATE
WINSLET

✳

Dress by Narciso Rodriquez

CLAIRE
DANES

✹

Dress by Nina Ricci

ANNE
HATHAWAY

✹

Dress by Azzaro

EVA LONGORIA
PARKER

✹

Dress by Jenny Packham

The Best of the Rest

ANGELINA
JOLIE

✳

Dress by Atelier Versace
Cannes Film Festival

HALLE
BERRY

✳

Dress by Marchesa
Shanghai International Film Festival

TAYLOR
SWIFT

✳

Dress by Angel Sanchez
Academy of Country Music Awar

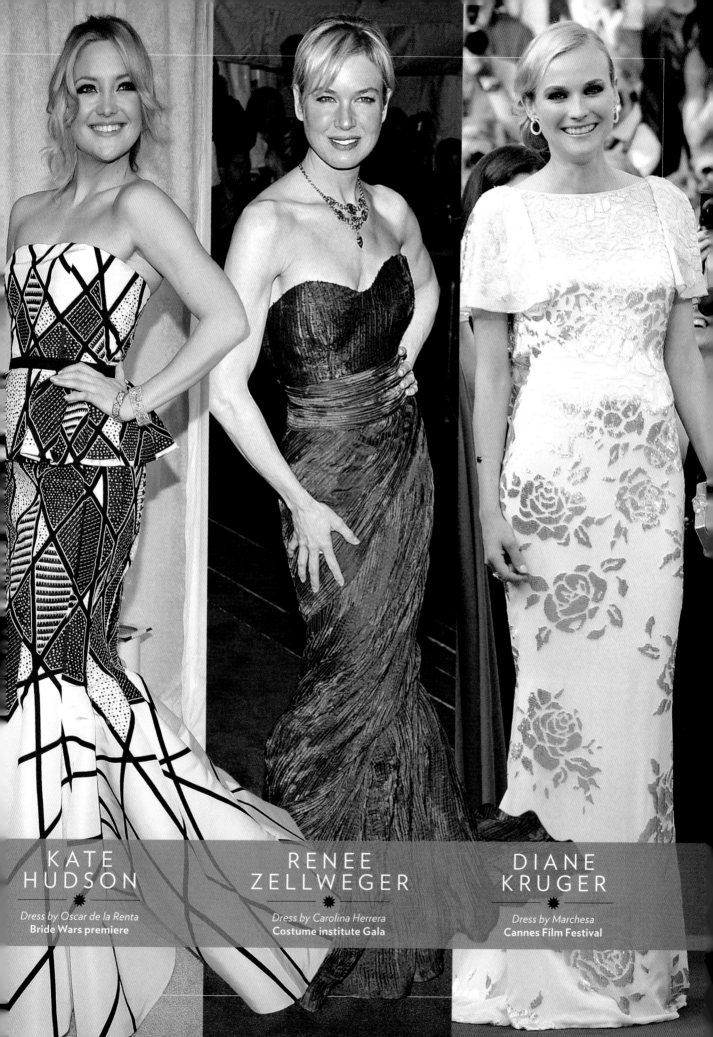

KATE
HUDSON
✳
Dress by Oscar de la Renta
Bride Wars premiere

RENEE
ZELLWEGER
✳
Dress by Carolina Herrera
Costume institute Gala

DIANE
KRUGER
✳
Dress by Marchesa
Cannes Film Festival

Worst Dressed

PAULA
ABDUL

✳

Aphrodite goes to the prom?

SANDRA
BULLOCK

✳

I said drape, not drapes!

LEIGHTON
MEESTER

✳

It's pants! It's a dress! It's . . . undecia

MADONNA

❋

Bugs Bunny's dominatrix fantasy?

HOLLY
MADISON

❋

Now available from Jackson Pollock couture!

TED KENNEDY
✱
AUGUST 25 | 1932-2009

Ted Kennedy never forgot a family birthday. So things seemed much as they should at the family compound in Hyannis Port, Mass., when Uncle Teddy wished his great-niece Michaela Cuomo a happy 12th on Aug. 25. Yet there were signs that Massachusetts' senior senator was taking a turn for the worse. For one, he was a day early with his birthday wishes. And earlier that morning his wife, Victoria Reggie Kennedy, 55, had told his close friend Sen. John Kerry, "This is the first day that he did not get out of bed." Around 9 p.m. Rev. Patrick Tarrant was summoned to Ted and Vicki's home. During Tarrant's previous visits, the senator had always led his Catholic clan in prayer. But on this night he left it to others as Vicki, son Ted Jr. and assorted relatives gathered around him. "He was not afraid to die," says Father Tarrant. "He told his family he was ready." Shortly before midnight, after a valiant 15-month battle with brain cancer, Edward Moore Kennedy passed away at age 77.

Farewell

Saying goodbye to Ted Kennedy, Farrah Fawcett, Patrick Swayze, Walter Cronkite, David Carradine, Ed McMahon, Natasha Richardson and more

EXUBERANT
Kennedy with son Patrick (right) and niece Rory on a roller coaster in 1976.

In the days that followed, the youngest of the glamorous Kennedy brothers was remembered as both a masterful politician who carried forward the progressive Kennedy promise and a patriarch who watched over the massive clan much like his father, Joe, had a generation before. During a funeral mass at the working-class Catholic church in Boston where the senator prayed when his daughter Kara, 49, battled lung cancer, President Barack Obama hailed Kennedy as "a champion for those who had none, the soul of the Democratic Party and the lion of the United States Senate." Though his achievements will be remembered, Obama said, "it is his giving heart that we will miss."

His turbulent life spanned youthful irresponsibility (he was, for instance, booted from Harvard for cheating on a Spanish exam), the assassinations of two brothers, a broken back from a plane crash and, when he was 37, the drowning of passenger Mary Jo Kopechne, 28, after Kennedy, who had been partying, drove his car off the tiny Chappaquiddick Bridge in Martha's Vineyard, Mass., and into a pond. What followed were years of building a legacy of public service in the U.S. Senate, where his name became synonymous with legislation on health care, education, civil rights and immigration. By the end of his nearly 47-year career, Kennedy could at times sway hearts, minds and votes on both sides of the aisle. His return to the Senate seven weeks after his May 2008 diagnosis of a brain tumor ensured the passage of a critical Medicare bill. At the funeral, after hailing Kennedy as "the greatest legislator of our time," Obama noted he was also "the friend and colleague who was always the first to pick up the phone and say, 'I'm sorry for your loss' or 'I hope you feel better.'"

At the service, Ted Jr., now 47, recalled a snowy day when he was 12 and trying to adjust to an artificial limb, having recently lost his right leg to bone cancer. Headed for the top of the family's steep driveway to sled, he said, "I slipped and I fell on the ice. And I started to cry, and I said, 'I can't do this.'" Gently, his father lifted him. "There is nothing that you can't do," he replied. "We're going to climb that hill together, even if it takes us all day." They did.

THREE PRINCES Teddy (with John and Robert in '60) was the only Kennedy brother who lived long enough to know his own grandchildren.

> "HE WAS THERE FOR ALL OF US, INCLUDING MY COUSINS WITHOUT A FATHER" —**NEPHEW ANTHONY SHRIVER**

KENNEDYS AHOY Teddy loved few things more than a family sail on his beloved boat *Mya*.

TOGETHER
Kennedy and second wife Vicki Reggie married in 1992. "It was Vicki's love," said a friend, "that made him comfortable in the world."

FARRAH FAWCETT
JUNE 25 | **1947 - 2009**

American Idol

*Saying goodbye to pop culture's
poster girl, an ineffable Angel*

For 2½ years, she fought cancer with everything she had. But Farrah Fawcett's final hours were peaceful ones. At her side in a Santa Monica hospital room, her longtime love Ryan O'Neal caressed her and recounted fond memories. "He talked to her continuously through the night," said Fawcett's doctor Lawrence Piro. "He professed his love to her, reviewed their relationship, told stories." Conscious until nearly the end, Fawcett "lit up when she heard those things."

Fawcett, 62, died on June 25. Like everything else in the TV icon's life, her illness became a public event, with paparazzi in pursuit and Fawcett herself recording her treatment for an NBC documentary, *Farrah's Story*. But if anyone understood the bizarre experience of fame, it was Fawcett, who found instant superstardom with the

PHENOMENON
Fawcett was as surprised as
anyone by Farrahmania:
"I didn't come to Los Angeles
expecting to be anything."

✳ **LIFE OF AN ANGEL** Farrah with Lee Majors in 1977 (left); Ryan O'Neal in 1990 (right); and her *Charlie's Angels* costars (below, with Jaclyn Smith, left, and Kate Jackson) during the show's '70s glory.

1976 premiere of *Charlie's Angels*.

With her tanned, toned, California look, she was, her manager said, "the female Robert Redford." In that brief moment, the shock wave of her fame was palpable; 12 million people—many, many of them teenage boys—bought her poster (still a record 30 years later). Even stepping out for dinner created a sensation. "We would go to Mr. Chow and a riot would break out over her in the streets," says her friend Joan Dangerfield. "They'd have to call the police. And she would be as nice to everyone as she could be. She had a heart as sweet as cotton candy."

Even while battling cancer, she found the strength to be kind, and optimistic. Said O'Neal: "She lost her hair. She lost weight. She just hadn't lost her hope."

> ## "FARRAH HAD A LOVE AFFAIR WITH THE CAMERA. SHE WAS JUST SO FULL OF SUNSHINE"
> —DIRECTOR HAL NEEDHAM

WALTER CRONKITE

JULY 17 | 1916-2009

When CBS News anchorman Walter Cronkite flew to Saigon in 1965 to see the Vietnam War up close, the military rolled out the red carpet. "They were determined to give him the grandest VIP treatment you can imagine," says *60 Minutes* correspondent Morley Safer. But after a week of airplane rides and rah-rah interviews, "we were sitting there having a drink, and he said, 'Now, what's the rest of the story?'" says Safer. "A lot of guys covering Vietnam didn't want to know what

was really going on. But Cronkite did. He wanted to know the truth."

Once he was satisfied he had facts in hand, Cronkite—at the time so trusted and familiar a part of American life that he was popularly known as Uncle Walter—had the power to move a nation. "Walter was always more than just an anchor," said President Barack Obama. "He was someone we could trust to guide us through the most important issues of the day; a voice of certainty in an uncertain world. He was family."

The son of a dentist, Cronkite decided to become

OVER THERE
Like many of TV news' first generation, Cronkite earned his stripes reporting from the front in WW II.

> "THE LAST TIME I HAD DINNER WITH HIM, HE SAID, 'I'VE GOT TO . . . BANG OUT SOME STORIES'" **—MORLEY SAFER**

a reporter after reading a short story in *American Boy* magazine and dropped out of the University of Texas during his junior year to cover state politics. In WW II he followed Allied forces in North Africa and Europe and, a decade later, joined CBS. "He came into television news in its infancy," says Katie Couric, who sits at the *CBS Evening News* desk today. "He believed in journalism and not opinion."

Indeed, Cronkite was so vigilant about presenting news objectively that most viewers had no idea whether he was a Republican or a Democrat (he was in fact an Independent). But when announcing President Kennedy's death in 1963, not even he could keep from choking back emotion. "There was something quite elegant about how he handled it," says Safer. "There was an Everyman's elegance about Walter: a sense of what the country aspires to be at its best."

CAPTAIN CRONKITE
The news ace was a passionate sailor and granddad.

PATRICK SWAYZE

SEPTEMBER 14 | 1952-2009

No matter what he was going through, Patrick Swayze never missed a chance to pay tribute to his wife of 34 years. So when Lisa Niemi turned 53 in May, the actor hosted a barbecue for friends and family at his ranch in the San Gabriel Mountains near L.A. Although he was battling pancreatic cancer, he remained as determined as ever. "His energy was, 'I'm going to beat this,'" recalled a friend, Bill Rotko. Yet, at the barbecue, "it was the first time you saw Patrick as you think of cancer patients," says Rotko. "He had switched from one chemo to another; it was a type of chemo he lost his hair with, and the fight was more obvious. If you judged a book by its cover . . . but you couldn't do that with Patrick Swayze because his energy was the opposite. He was a strong guy."

On Sept. 14, after a 20-month battle, Swayze, 57, died at home with Lisa by his side. A classically trained ballet dancer who became a movie leading man, "Patrick was a rare and beautiful combination of raw masculinity and amazing grace," said his *Dirty Dancing* costar Jennifer Grey. A high school football player who could pull off gravity-defying grand jetés, a big-screen heartthrob who drove his own cattle, Swayze brought his almost paradoxical talents to huge hits like 1987's *Dancing* and 1990's *Ghost*. "He lived 100 lifetimes in one," said Rob Lowe, who costarred with him in 1983's *The Outsiders*. Adds choreographer Kenny Ortega: "He had such an enthusiasm for everything he did. If he could climb it, he climbed it. If he could write it, he wrote it. If he could dance it . . . well, we all knew he did. He lived."

LIKE SO
Prepping for *Dirty Dancing*, Swayze (with Jennifer Grey) rehearsed with his wife, dancer Lisa Niemi.

"I NEVER SAW HIM IN A BAD MOOD. . . . HE GOT THE HUGEST KICK OUT OF SEEING OTHER PEOPLE SMILE" —A FRIEND

FEAT OF CLAY
As the title character of *Ghost*, Swayze (with Demi Moore) shaped pots and made women weak.

NATASHA RICHARDSON

✳

MARCH 18 | 1963-2009

At first it seemed like nothing. On vacation in Canada, actress Natasha Richardson, 45, took a ski lesson and tumbled on a beginners' run. "Two ski-patrol officers came down and checked her out," said a resort spokesperson. "She was lucid, talking, even making jokes." They advised her to see a doctor; she declined.

Brought to her hotel room an hour later, "she was walking," said the spokesperson. "She didn't have any signs of impact. Then just all of a sudden, she started to suffer headaches, and the instructor said, 'Okay, you better go to the hospital,' and she agreed."

Her condition worsened with alarming speed. Medically nothing seemed to help. She died two days later; an autopsy showed she had suffered a fatal epidural hematoma, bleeding between her brain and skull. Her husband, actor Liam Neeson, 56, and children, Micheal, 13, and Daniel, 12, were devastated. "The loss of Tasha . . . leaves a gaping hole in many of our lives," said Mia Farrow, a close friend. "There is nothing she would not do for her friends 24-7. That's rare."

✸ ED McMAHON

JUNE 23 | **1923-2009**

FOR ED McMAHON, SERVING AS TV's most famous second banana had tremendous appeal. "It takes a talent all its own, like being a catcher," said McMahon, who spent 30 years introducing Johnny Carson on *The Tonight Show* and serving as his straight man in countless sketches. "It's your job to absorb what's thrown because, in the final analysis, he's the guy who has to throw the ball."

It was more than a role. "Ed is what you see up there," said Carson, who died in 2005. "He's the same guy off as he is on." A decorated combat pilot in the Korean War, McMahon rose through a series of TV and radio jobs before starting on *Tonight* in 1962. Fiercely entrepreneurial, he moonlighted as a ubiquitous pitchman and hosted the talent show *Star Search* for 12 years.

Toward the end, he battled health problems but kept his perspective. "You can have 15 pairs of shoes; you can only wear one," McMahon, who died at 86, once said. "But friends, you can have as many as you can handle. I don't mind dying; the part I'll miss is my friends."

> "I DON'T
> MIND DYING;
> THE PART
> I'LL MISS
> IS MY
> FRIENDS"

✳ BEA ARTHUR

APRIL 25 | 1922-2009

BEA ARTHUR COULD GET LAUGHS with the flick of her wrist, or a withering glare. "How she held on to an audience was a wonder," said Norman Lear, who produced her groundbreaking 1970s sitcom *Maude*. "She got roars just shifting her weight." The no-nonsense Arthur—who died of cancer at age 86—chalked that success up to hard labor and a little luck. "I'd been working my ass off onstage for 25 years," she told PEOPLE in 1999. When *Maude* turned her, overnight, into a star at 50, it made her feel "like a middle-aged Cinderella."

Ironically, she was a Cinderella who, as the star of a show with a bracingly feminist bent, was also "a symbol of what women were fighting for," said Lear. Her own battle ended in her L.A. home, surrounded by her family, including sons Daniel and Matthew. "We will never see her like again," said *Desperate Housewives* creator Marc Cherry, who had been a writer on Arthur's second sitcom hit, *The Golden Girls*. "She was the last of the great broads."

David Carradine was a man of extremes. A hard-drinking hippie who once vandalized a neighbor's house while naked and high, he could also seem, at times, as spiritual as the Shaolin monk in his hit '70s television series *Kung Fu*. And in the final weeks of his life, Carradine, 72, seemed to be a man at peace. "He was definitely on a real high note," said his friend, kung fu master Rob Moses. "He sounded like an airborne dolphin."

But there was still a dark side, or, at least, a bizarre side. On June 4, a maid found Carradine hanging naked in the closet of his hotel room in Bangkok, where he had been shooting a film. A medical examiner ruled out suicide; other details—Carradine had cords tied around his wrists, neck and genitals—gave rise to speculation that he accidentally died during an autoerotic act. (Ex-wife Gail Jensen said that the five-times married actor did, indeed, have a penchant for tying himself up.)

Carradine's family chose to remember the father of seven's passionate life rather than the way he died. "He had a rough exterior, but he had a really sweet core," said brother Bruce Carradine, 76. "He had an amazing amount of confidence. We all loved him." Given his colorful past, Carradine might actually have been amused by all the headlines. Said actor Michael Madsen, a long-time pal: "You don't expect someone like David to die in his sleep."

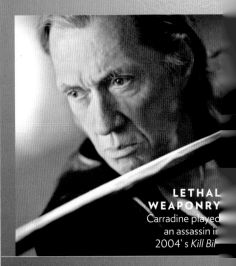

LETHAL WEAPONRY Carradine played an assassin in 2004' s *Kill Bill*

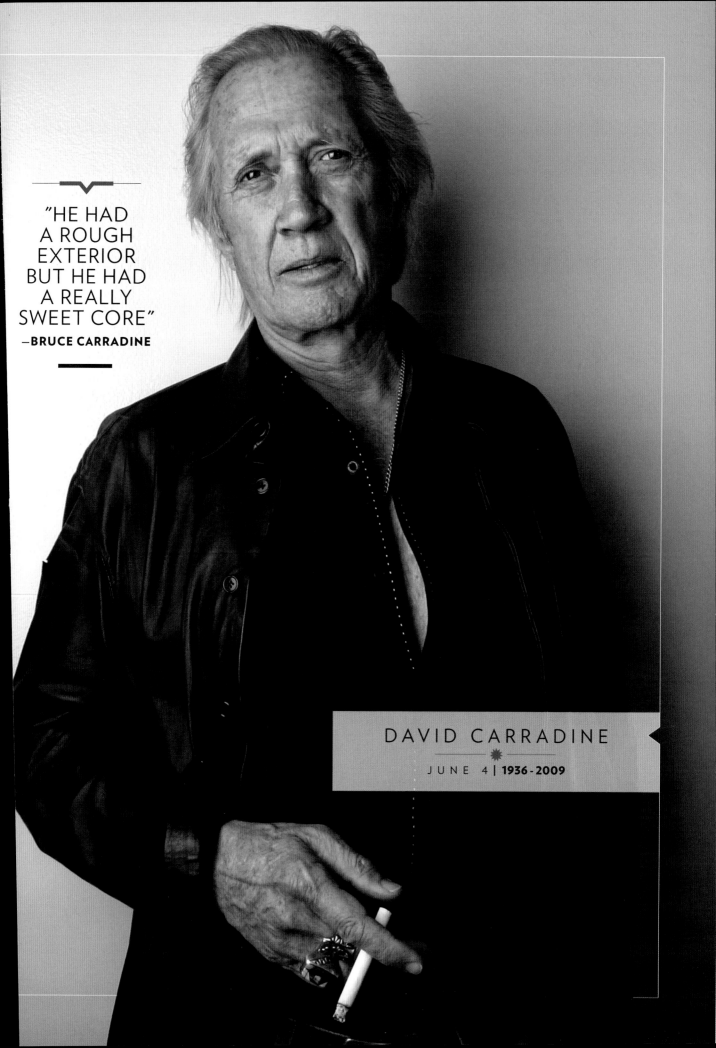

"HE HAD
A ROUGH
EXTERIOR
BUT HE HAD
A REALLY
SWEET CORE"
—BRUCE CARRADINE

DAVID CARRADINE

JUNE 4 | 1936-2009

DJ AM
✸
AUGUST 28 | **1973-2009**

Eleven months earlier, Adam Goldstein had jumped through flames to survive a Learjet crash; two of his friends didn't make it. That experience left Goldstein—better known as DJ AM—covered in severe burns and keenly aware of how lucky he was. "I live my life to the fullest," he said afterward, "[because] I don't know how much longer I'm going to be around."

Weeks before the anniversary of the crash, Goldstein, 36, was found dead in his New York City apartment. Having ended his relationship with his girlfriend earlier in the week, he Tweeted an ominous Grandmaster Flash lyric on Aug. 25: "New York, New York, big city of dreams/ And everything in New York ain't always what it seems." The police found the recovering drug addict (in July he said he'd been sober for more than 11 years) in bed with a half-used bag of crack cocaine and two pipes three days later. Prescription pills lay nearby. Friends says Goldstein was not depressed about his breakup, but that the survivor's guilt and post-traumatic stress disorder he battled as a result of the crash may have contributed to a relapse. "His death," said one friend, "was the direct result of the plane crash."

TEEN TITAN
Hughes (with *Sixteen Candles*' Molly Ringwald and Michael Schoeffling) captured the goofy wonder of adolescence.

✸ JOHN HUGHES
AUGUST 6 | 1950 - 2009

ONE OF THE 1980S' most influential filmmakers, Hughes crafted hit after coming-of-age hit, including *Sixteen Candles, The Breakfast Club* and *Ferris Bueller's Day Off*, forever defining what it meant to be a teen in suburbia. "He knew teenagers because he was one himself," said Kelly LeBrock, star of his 1985 comedy *Weird Science*. "He was always running around with high-top sneakers with no laces in them."

Hughes, who died of a heart attack at 59, never cared much for Hollywood, leaving it behind in the '90s for the Midwest, where he set many of his films. The director, survived by his wife of 39 years, Nancy, and two grown sons, did what many of his movies' grown-ups didn't—spent time with his kids. While filming *Pretty in Pink,* "he'd invite me over to the house and they'd all be jumping around the pool," said James Spader. "He protected them, and I think that's why he left Hollywood."

✸ EUNICE SHRIVER
AUGUST 11 | 1921 - 2009

MATRIARCH
Shriver with daughter Maria and son-in-law Arnold Schwarzenegger in 1994.

GIVEN TO PUFFING THIN BLACK CIGARS and speaking her mind, Eunice Shriver, 86, could be daunting. But as the fifth of nine children in the legendary Kennedy brood, Eunice was no more demanding of others than she was of herself. "If you don't have an idea that materializes and changes a person's life, then what have you got?" Shriver said in a 2006 interview. "You have talk."

The guiding idea in Shriver's life was to open doors—athletic, medical, social—for people who needed help. To that end, in 1968 she launched the Special Olympics. There were 1,000 competitors; today, 3 million hopefuls from more than 180 countries vie to compete. "Throughout her extraordinary life she touched the lives of millions," said her brother, Sen. Ted Kennedy, "and for Eunice that was never enough."

EDITOR Cutler Durkee **DESIGN DIRECTOR** Sara Williams **DIRECTOR OF PHOTOGRAPHY** Chris Dougherty **ART DIRECTOR** Cass Spencer **DESIGNER** Margarita Mayoral **PHOTO EDITOR** C. Tiffany Lee-Ramos **EDITORIAL MANAGER** Andrew Abrahams **WRITERS** Chuck Arnold, Steve Dougherty, Tom Gliatto, Allison Lynn, Alex Tresniowski **REPORTERS** Joyce Chen, Jeremy Gordon, Daniel Levy, Debra Lewis-Boothman, Hugh McCarten, Lesley Messer, Gail Nussbaum, Thailan Pham, Jane Sugden **COPY EDITORS** Ben Harte (Chief), James Bradley, Pearl Chen, Gabrielle Danchick, Aura Davies, Alan Levine, Amanda Pennelly, Mary C. Radich, Jennifer Shotz **PRODUCTION EDITOR** Ilsa Enomoto **SCANNERS** Brien Foy, Stephen Pabarue **IMAGING** Fran Fitzgerald (Imaging Director), Rob Roszkowski (Imaging Manager), Romeo Cifelli, Charles Guardino (Imaging Production Managers), Jeff Ingledue **SPECIAL THANKS TO** Céline Wojtala, David Barbee, Jane Bealer, Stacie Fenster, Margery Frohlinger, Ean Sheehy, Patrick Yang

TIME INC. HOME ENTERTAINMENT
PUBLISHER Richard Fraiman **GENERAL MANAGER** Steven Sandonato **EXECUTIVE DIRECTOR, MARKETING SERVICES** Carol Pittard **DIRECTOR, RETAIL & SPECIAL SALES** Tom Mifsud **DIRECTOR, NEW PRODUCT DEVELOPMENT** Peter Harper **ASSISTANT DIRECTOR, BOOKAZINE MARKETING** Laura Adam **ASSISTANT PUBLISHING DIRECTOR, BRAND MARKETING** Joy Butts **ASSOCIATE COUNSEL** Helen Wan **BOOK PRODUCTION MANAGER** Suzanne Janso **DESIGN & PREPRESS MANAGER** Anne-Michelle Gallero **BRAND & LICENSING MANAGER** Alexandra Bliss **ASSISTANT BRAND MANAGER** Melissa Joy Kong
SPECIAL THANKS TO Christine Austin, Glenn Buonocore, Jim Childs, Susan Chodakiewicz, Rose Cirrincione, Jacqueline Fitzgerald, Lauren Hall, Jennifer Jacobs, Brynn Joyce, Robert Marasco, Amy Migliaccio, Brooke Reger, Dave Rozzelle, Ilene Schreider, Adriana Tierno, Alex Voznesenskiy, Sydney Webber, Jonathan White

ISBN 10: 1-60320-098-3, ISBN 13: 978-1-60320-098-1, ISSN: 1522-5895 Copyright © 2009 Time Inc. Home ENTERTAINMENT. Published by People Books, Time Inc., 1271 Avenue of the Americas, New York, N.Y. 10020. All rights reserved. No part of this book may be reproduced in any form or by any electronic or mechanical means, including information storage and retrieval systems, without permission in writing from the publisher, except by a reviewer, who may quote brief passages in a review. People Books is a trademark of Time Inc. We welcome your comments and suggestions about People Books. **Please write to us at People Books**, Attention: Book Editors, P.O. Box 11016, Des Moines, IA 50336-1016. ● If you would like to order any of our hardcover Collector's Edition books, please call us at 1-800-327-6388 (Monday through Friday, 7 a.m.-8 p.m., or Saturday, 7 a.m.-6 p.m. Central Time).

Credits

FRONT COVER
(clockwise from top right)
Lance Staedler/Corbis Outline;
Dan Cappellazzo/Polaris; Carlos
Barria/Reuters; UPI/Landov;
Kevin Mazur/Wireimage;
Nebinger-Orban/Abaca USA

CONTENTS
2-3 (clockwise from top left) Kevin
Winter/Getty Images; Reed Saxon/
AP; CBS/Landov; Jeff Sciortino/
MJT/Admedia; Stephen Danelian;
Jonathan Ernst/Reuters

NEWSMAKERS
4-5 Chip Somodevilla/Corbis;
6 Chang W. Lee/The New York
Times/Redux; **7** (from top)
Chuck Kennedy/Reuters; Kevin
Lamarque/Reuters(2);
8 Pete Souza/White House;
9 (clockwise from bottom right)
Mikhail Klimentyev/Ria Novosti/
EPA; Larry Downing/Reuters;
Pete Souza/White House(2);
10 Greg Allen/Retna; **12** (clockwise
from left) Monica Almeida/The New
York Times/Redux; Scott Olson/
Getty Images; The Plain Dealer/
Landov; **13** Julien Hekimian/
Wireimage; **14** Michael Pilla/TLC/
Getty Images; **16** Kris Ingraham/AP;
17 (from top) Courtesy
Travolta Family/Rogers & Cowan/
Reuters; SDFL/Splash News(2);
18 (from top) Ruby Washington/
The New York Times/Redux;
Eugene Gologursky/Getty Images
for Sony Cierge; Lucy Nicholson/
Reuters; Mary Altaffer/AP;
19 (clockwise from top left)
William Carl Probyn/Zuma Press;
People; Karl Mondon/Bay Area
News Group/Zuma Press; Deano/
Splash News; El Dorado County
Sheriff's Dept./AP; **20** Steven
Day/AP; **21** Nigel Parry/CPi;
22 (top) Meet the Famous;
23 Ken Mckay/Rex USA;
24 (top) David Zalubowski/AP;

25 TTA Media/Splash News;
26 (clockwise from left) L.Cohen/
Wireimage; Anchorage Daily News/
MCT/Landov; Al Grillo/AP(2);
27 Al Grillo/AP; **28** Rex USA;
29 (clockwise from top) U.S.
Navy/Zuma Press; Alison Redlich/
Burlington Free Press/Polaris; Eric
Thayer/Reuters

ANIMALS
30 Perez-Daniel/INF; **31** (clockwise
from bottom left) Ramey; Daryl
Wright/Newspix; **32** Gary Rothstein/
EPA; **33** (from top) Damian
Dovarganes/AP; Splash News

CRIME
34-35 (from left) CBS/AP; Lori
Shepler/Getty Images; Lester
Cohen/Wireimage; **36-37**
(clockwise from bottom left) INF;
Anthony Dixon/Wenn; Alan Zale/
The New York Times/Redux; Schuler
Family/AP; Newsday/MCT/Landov;
38 (from left) Daniele La Monaca/
Reuters; Rex USA; Stefano Medici/
AP; **39** (from top) Karena Cawthon/
The Pensacola News Journal/AP;
Escambia Sheriff's Dept./AP(2)

WEDDINGS
40-41 Larry Busacca/AM/Contour
by Getty Images(2); **42** Justine
Ungaro-Sota Dzine/Studio Thisis;
43 Blake/Splash News; **44** Pacific
Coast News; **45** (from top) Kevin
Perkins/Pacific Coast News; Pacific
Coast News; **46** Andrew H.Walker/
Getty Images; **47** Gilbert Flores/
Celebrity Photo; **48** (from top)
Alex Whistler/Retna; Venturini/
Bauer-Griffin; **49** Donna Newman;
50 Bertrand Rindoff-Petroff/AP; **51**
Kevin Mazur/Wireimage; **52** Brian
Marcus/Fred Marcus Photography;
53 (from top) Getty Images; Wenn;
54 (from top) Louise Barnsley-Kevin
Perkins/Pacific Coast News; Flynet;
55 Todd G.-John K./Splash News

BABIES
56 Robin Layton/AP; **58** Peter
Yang/August; **59** Jeff Vespa/
Getty Images; **60** Dom Furore/
Courtesy Woods Family; **62** Jackson
Lee/Splash News; **63** Jeff Vespa/
Wireimage; **64** Justin Coit;
66 Derek Blanks/Hilton Media
Group; **67** Sam Sharma/Pacific
Coast News; **68** Kurt Iswarienko;
70 Cheyenne Ellis/AP; **71** (from left)
Flynet; Peter Yang/August

BODY
72-73 Stephen Danelian(2);
74 (from top) Mario Anzuoni/Reuters;
WG/Flynet; **75** Stephen Danelian;
76 Brian Doben; **77** (clockwise from
top right) X 17; Paul Harris/Pacific
Coast News; Brian Doben

SPLITS
78 Ron Sachs-CNP/Photolink,
80-81 (from left) Francis Specker/
Landov; S.Granitz/Wireimage;
FayesVision/Wenn; **82** Art Seitz/
KPA/Zuma News; **83** Albert
Michael/Startraks; **84** Chris Whittle/
Splash News; **85** Michael Buckner/
Getty Images; **86** Kevin Mazur/
Wireimage; **87** (from top) Rex USA;
John Shearer/Wireimage

MOVIES
88 Ishika Mohan/Fox Searchlight;
90-91 (clockwise from top left)
Disney/Pixar; Frank Masi/Warner
Bros.; Paramount/AP; Jamie
Trueblood/Paramount; **92-93**
(clockwise from top right) Kimberley
French/Summit Entertainment(2);
Richard Cartwright/Columbia
Pictures; David Giesbrecht/Sony
Pictures; **94-95** (clockwise from top
left) Sam Emerson/Disney;
Industrial Light & Magic/Paramount;
Frank Masi/Disney; Kerry Brown/
Sony Pictures Classics

TV
96 Michael Thomas; **98** Justin
Lubin/Courtesy NBCU (insets from

top) Mitchell Haaseth/Courtesy
NBCU; Virginia Sherwood/Courtesy
NBCU; **99** (clockwise from top)
Matthias Clamer/Fox; Courtesy
Fox News; Dylan Martinez/Reuters;
100 Byron Cohen/Courtesy NBCU;
101(clockwise from middle right)
Kristin Callahan/Acepixs; Frank
Micelotta/Getty Images; Gary
Lewis/Retna; Vivian Zink/ABC/
Getty Images

MUSIC
102-103 Melanie Dunea/CPi;
(inset) Gary Hershorn/Reuters;
104 Jim Cooper/AP; **105** (from top)
Jay Brooks/Retna; PA Empics/Abaca
USA; Harmonix/MTV Games/
Reuters; **106** (clockwise from top
left) Kevin
Mazur/Wireimage; Robb Cohen/
Retna; **107** El-Jeremy Cowart/Getty
Images for Jive Records;
108 (clockwise from top left) EJC/
ADD/Starmax; Seth Browarnik/
Startraks; Demis Maryannakis/
Splash News; John Kennedy/Splash
News; **109** (clockwise from top
left) Bauer-Griffin; Darrin Zammit
Lupi/Reuters; Frank Micelotta/
PictureGroup; Meeno/Courtesy
Interscope

FASHION
110 Mario Anzuoni/Reuters;
112-113 (from left) Marc Larkin/LFI;
Jean Paul Aussenard/Broadimage;
Fernando Allende/Broadimage;
Jean Paul Aussenard/Broadimage;
Gilbert Flores/Celebrity Photo;
Digital Focus Intl/Empics
Entertainment/Abaca USA;
114-115 (from left) Visual
Press; Lionel Hahn/Abaca USA;
Gregg Deguire/PictureGroup;
Mathew Imaging/Wireimage;
FayesVision/Wenn; Axelle/
Bauer-Griffin; **116-117** (from
left) Danny Moloshok/Reuters;
Dan MacMedan/Wireimage; Jon
Kopaloff/Filmmagic; Goff/INF;
Steve Granitz/Wireimage; Kevin

Mazur/Wireimage; **118-119** (from
left) Chris Delmas/Visual Press(2);
Gilbert Flores/Celebrity Photo;
Jason Merritt/Getty Images;
Lisa Rose Photography(2);
120-121 (from left) Jason Merritt/
Getty Images; Peter Brooker/
Rex USA; Goff/INF; Lisa Rose
Photography(3); **122-123** (from
left) Nebinger-Orban/Abaca
USA; Andrew Ross/Getty Images;
Jason Merritt/Getty Images;
Dimitrios Kambouris/Wireimage;
RD-Dzieken/Retna; Pete Mariner/
Retna; **124-125** (from left) Jon
Kopaloff/Wireimage; Sara De Boer/
Retna; Stephen Lovekin/Getty
Images; Brian Zak/Sipa; Sam Morris/
Getty Images

TRIBUTES
126 Joseph Dennehy/Boston
Globe/Landov; **128** (from top) AP;
Ken Regan/Camera 5; **129** John
Tlumacki/Boston Globe/Landov;
130 Douglas Kirkland/Corbis;
132 Douglas Kirkland/Corbis;
133 (clockwise from top left) Ron
Galella/Wireimage; CBS/Landov;
Photofest; **134** CBS/Landov;
135 (from top) Bettmann/Corbis;
Kelly-Mooney Photography;Corbis;
136 Herbie Knott/Rex USA;
137 (from top) Photofest; Globe;
138 Robert Ashcroft/CPi; **139**
Globe; **140** (from left) Photofest;
Everett; **141** Mark Mainz/Getty
Images; **142** Patrick Hoelck/Contour
by Getty Images; **143** (from top)
MPTV; Ron Galella/Wireimage

BACK COVER
(clockwise from top left) MPTV;
Gustavo Caballero/Getty Images;
Peter Kramer/AP; MAP-AVM/
Splash News; Michael Pilla/TLC/
Getty Images; The Orange County
Register/Zuma Press; Courtesy
Disney; Ken Mckay/Rex USA;
Stephen Danelian; Ken Regan/
Camera 5